Robert Gordon Latham

Two Dissertations on the Hamlet of Saxo Grammaticus and of Shakespear

I. The historical personality of Hamlet. II. The relation of the Hamlet of Shakespear

to the German play, Prinz Hamlet aus Dänemark, etc.

Robert Gordon Latham

Two Dissertations on the Hamlet of Saxo Grammaticus and of Shakespear
I. The historical personality of Hamlet. II. The relation of the Hamlet of Shakespear to the German play, Prinz Hamlet aus Dänemark, etc.

ISBN/EAN: 9783337319533

Printed in Europe, USA, Canada, Australia, Japan

Cover: Foto ©Thomas Meinert / pixelio.de

More available books at **www.hansebooks.com**

TWO DISSERTATIONS

ON THE

HAMLET

OF

SAXO GRAMMATICUS

AND OF

SHAKESPEAR.

I. THE HISTORICAL PERSONALITY OF HAMLET.
II. THE RELATION OF THE 'HAMLET' OF
SHAKESPEAR TO THE GERMAN PLAY,
'PRINZ HAMLET AUS DÄNEMARK,' ETC.

BY

R. G. LATHAM, M.A., M.D., ETC.

WILLIAMS AND NORGATE,

14, HENRIETTA STREET, COVENT GARDEN, LONDON,

AND 20, SOUTH FREDERICK STREET, EDINBURGH.

1872.

ON THE DOUBLE PERSONALITY OF THE HAMLET OF SAXO GRAMMATICUS—THE HAMLET OF SHAKESPEAR—ITS RELATION TO THE GERMAN HAMLET.

BY DR. R. G. LATHAM, M.A., M.D., ETC.

PART I.

SAXO GRAMMATICUS lived in Denmark during the latter half of the twelfth century, and wrote a work on the history of his country,—the 'Historia Danica;' his friend, patron, and instigator being Absalon, Archbishop of Lund. His father and grandfather held respectable offices in the state. He was born not much before, nor yet long after, 1150. His work was begun after 1177. Little as this information amounts to, it is nearly all we have; nor is this little absolutely beyond cavil. It has even been doubted, for instance, whether he were a native of Denmark, the name *Saxo* suggesting a German origin. It seems, however, to have passed into a proper name before the end of the eleventh century. When it took the honourable addition of *Grammaticus* is uncertain.

Of authorities, in the strict sense of the term, Saxo quotes only two,—Beda and Dudo of St. Quentin, both incidentally. He made, however, application to the learned men of the day, and resorted to the traditionary lore of the Icelanders. Thirdly, he quotes certain passages from certain poets, but, as

B

they are in Latin and anonymous, the value of them
is uncertain.   Are they originals or translations?
They occur chiefly in the earlier books.   His cotemporary Snorro Sturleson, in his 'Heimskringla,' or
'History of the Kings of Norway,' written in the
vernacular Icelandic, makes similar references.   His
quotations, however, are in the original language and
the original metres, and generally the name of the
composers accompanies them.   Upon the whole,
then, we have a fair general notion of what Saxo
means by the *carmina antiqua*.   Occasionally we
can trace them in the prose narrative by their
alliteration.

The true illustration, however, of Saxo is to be
found in the age to which he belonged.   Neither he
nor his cotemporaries had anything like systematic,
critical, or adequately informed predecessors.   In the
way of actual testimony they had nothing but that of
the men of their own generation for the events of their
own time.   Application to the oldest of these cotemporaries led them generally into the region of tradition.   Latin accounts, when they delivered new
matter, would rarely transcend the introduction of
Christianity; even the *carmina antiqua* would generally consist of allusions to events supposed to be
generally known rather than of explicit narratives.

About any English sources Saxo says nothing beyond his reference to Beda.   The only parts, however, of the earlier narrative which point in the
direction of genuine history are English.   This is
because occasionally, exceptionally, and under very
favourable circumstances, an event or individual may
be common to the history of two nations, of which the

records of the one are older than those of the other, but at the same time accessible to the younger. When such happens, a piece of real or approximate history may be obtained. If so, it stands by itself, isolated, and, as such, contrasted with what precedes and what follows it. This is the way in which the Britons knew about Cassivelaunus, Cynobelinus, and the like; not because there were any native records to say who they were and what they did, but because certain Romans had written about them, and certain Britons had read what they wrote. Beyond all this, there were certain floating names, narratives, and inferences wearing the garb of tradition, of which the best that could be said is that where there is a superstructure there is a foundation, or, more simply, where there is smoke there is fire.

Saxo's age, however, either required or produced something more than this; for it was the age of the early French romances, the age of poems in Germany like the 'Nibelungen-lied,' the age of a wholly new literature in the vernacular languages, and of certain very peculiar and characteristic forms of Latin prose. They passed for history; logography, however, would be the better name. That any writer willingly and consciously sat down to concoct a systematic series of dynasties with the view of extending the antiquity of his county to such or such Scriptural or Classical date, is what few believe; but that sooner or later most countries produced a work in which such an extension is to be found, is beyond doubt; and one of these is the 'Historia Danica,' another being the 'British History' of Geoffrey of Monmouth. There are others, but these best illustrate both one another and the age which produced them.

We may call this constructive chronology; though I again guard myself against the supposition that I consider either Geoffrey or Saxo as wilful and conscious constructors. How the system grew up is doubtful. It culminated, however, in more countries than one about the same time, — the time under notice.

How it grew we cannot say; but now that we have got it, we can analyse it.

The common-sense method of treating lists of kings which logographies of this kind give us is to take the two extremes, either of which supplies us with a starting-point. We know that the newest is historical; we know that the earliest is not. We may begin, in British history, with Cassivelaunus and the evidence of Julius Cæsar, or we may begin with Brutus, the eponymus of Britain, and no evidence whatsoever.

This principle is universal in its application, though it need not always be applied. Sometimes we see all that it gives us by mere inspection; at others, it has special complications that keep it in the background. It is always, however, implied. In the following series the most historical part lies near the middle. The thirty-eighth king is a cotemporary of Charlemagne; and, as this brings him on the confines of continuous history, the list is here made to end with him.

1. *Humble I.* (word for word *Hamblet.*)
2. Dan I.
3. *Humble II.* (*vide supra*) and Lother.
4. Skiold.
5. Gram.
6. *Guthorm* and Hading.
7. *Frotho I.*
8. *Halfdan.*

9. Roe.
10. Scato.
11. Helgo.
12. *Rolvo.*
13. Hother.
14. *Röricus.*
15. *Vikletus.*
16. *Vermundus.*
17. *Uffo.*
18. Dan II.
19. HUGLETUS (*melius* HU-
    GLEKUS).
20. Frotho II.
21. Fridlev.
22. Frotho III.
23. Frotho IV.

24. *Ingeld.*
25. Frotho V.
26. *Haldan.*
27. *Sivald.*
28. *Sigurd.*
29. Five Kings.
30. Harold Hildetand.
31. Olo.
32. Omundus.
33. Syvardus.
34. Buthlus.
35. Jarmeríc.
36. Snio.
37. Gormo.
38. *Götrícus.*

To these must be added, from the Danish dynasties in Ireland, *Amblaibh Cuaran*, or *Anlaf Cwiran*, and from the kings of Norway, *Olaf Kyrre.*

Now it is not in accordance with the rules of rhetoric to address the argument to the eye rather than the understanding, and to throw the proper duties of the writer upon the printer. Nevertheless, it is clear that in the preceding list a great deal is indicated by the italics. This is, firstly, because the question is so complicated that no means whatever of abating its complexity should be neglected; and secondly, because a general view of the import of several names separated from one another by occasional intervals is absolutely necessary as a preliminary. *Hugletus* has a value of its own. *Vikletus, Vermundus, Uffo* have theirs. The others, in italic, have theirs; and, in a smaller degree, every name on the list has a value of some kind or other.

The reasons for the predominance of the italicized names are as follow. They apply to persons who are mentioned in compositions other than Scandinavian, and as such have a prerogative claim to something like historical value. Anglo-Saxon England notices *Guthorm*, *Halfdan*, *Frotho*, and *Ingeld*, so that we find these names on both sides of the German Ocean. But the Anglo-Saxon history is, for the time, obscure. Of one of the two, either *Sigurd* or *Sivald*, or (more probably) a mixture of the two, there are notices in both the German and English literatures; and, though neither of these is absolutely authoritative, the concurrence of the evidence is better than no secondary confirmation at all. Of Rolvo and Röricus more will be said hereafter. The remaining names, as far as Sigurd, which are printed in ordinary type, are only found in the Old Norse narratives, Norwegian, Swedish, or Icelandic, which differ from those of Denmark only in degree. Between Sigurd and Götricus the bearing of the names upon the present argument is less direct.

Now *Vikletus*, *Vermundus*, and *Uffo* are names of which the slightly altered forms *Wiglaf*, *Wærmund*, and *Offa* appear in the Anglo-Saxon poem ' Beowulf,' where they belong to men of the same generation; herein giving us a slight deviation from the text of Saxo, where they are grandfather, son, and grandson respectively. This, however, has never induced a single commentator to hesitate in identifying them. They differ, too, in the details of their history. Nevertheless their connection has always been allowed. Nor is this strange, provided that we do not take it for more than it is worth. It is not supposed that

an accurate history can be got either out of the
'Historia Danica' or the poem of 'Beowulf,' nor yet
out of the two combined. It is only believed that
the same characters are to be found, to a considerable extent, in both. And surely this is the case;
for, besides these, the names of Halfdan, Frotho (one
or more), and Ingeld are common to the two compositions. Still Viklet, Vermund, and Uffo have the
prerogative. They are most closely connected with one
another, not only in Saxo's history and the poem,
but elsewhere. They appear in more than one of
the Anglo-Saxon genealogies, and here, as in Saxo,
in sequence rather than as mere cotemporaries.

The order in the genealogies is (1) Wiglaf, (2)
Wærmund, (3) Offa, and that wherever we find the
names. More than this, in two English biographies
of King Offa, of which more will be said as we proceed, the name of Offa and Vermund reappear, and
in the local traditions of Warwickshire they appear
again. On the other hand it is only in Saxo that
they are connected with either Hamlet or Röric. In
'Beowulf' Wiglaf appears to be the youngest of the
three, and Wærmund the oldest. They are not, however, as in Saxo, father, son, and grandson, though
this (be it noted) is what they are in the genealogies.

Upon the name *Hugletus* so much depends that
we must begin with putting it into its right form,
by changing the *t* into *k*. In doing this we merely
follow our predecessors, the earlier of whom had less
evidence in favour of the change than has since been
supplied by the later ones. The same is the case
with the *t* in Vikletus, and something very like it
with the *th* of Amle*th*us.

Laying aside the manifestly erroneous Huhle*sth*, we have the four following forms,—(1, 2) Hugle*k* and Hugle*g*, (3) Hugla*f*, and (4) Hugle*t*, the last being, decidedly, the worst. It is found, as we see, in Saxo; it is also found in two of his successors, the author of the 'Chronicon Erici Regis,' and Petrus Olaus; but it is found nowhere else. Huthle*f*, too, is found but once. In all the other lists the spelling is either with a *k* or a *g*.

(v.)

Roric Slaganbogi.	Uffi.
Wiglaff.	Dan.
Wermund.	*Huglekr.*
Frothi hin Frökni.	

(vi.)

Röric Slanggenbögi.	Vffa.
Vinglet.	Dan.
Ouermund Blinde.	*Huglekr.*
Frothi hin Frökni.	

(vii.)[1]

Dan.	Hughlek.
Frothi.	

Thirdly, there is, in Saxo himself, a second Hugle*tus*, a king of Ireland. The story, however, which is told of him is one which reappears in the 'Heimskringla.' There he is a king of Sweden, and Huhlei*kr* is his name. Saxo's form, then, is a bad qne; so that, as a great deal depends upon it, it is fortunate that it is so easily corrected.

Now, for more than half a century it has been

---

[1] The numerals are those of the divisions in the first volume of Langebek's 'Scriptores.' Roric is here contemporary with Röricus, who is contemporary with Amlethus; Uffo is wanting; but Vermund is blind. See pp. 5—and 70, 71.

acknowledged that, word for word, this *Huhleikr* is the Norse form of the Anglo-Saxon *Hygelác*, or *Higelác*, one of the heroes in 'Beowulf,' and (what is more important) that both are, word for word, *Chochilaicus*, or *Chochelagus*, the name of a Danish sea-king who, in the beginning of the sixth century, was killed in the Netherlands,—the authority being no less than that of Gregory of Tours, whose important work on the early history of the Franks was composed within sixty years of the event.[2]

This brings us to the high and exceptional value assigned to the name *Huglet*, or, in the full Latin form, *Hugletus*; for upon this name, along with the assumptions that connect it with another, nine-tenths of the present argument depends.

"His gestis, Dani cum rege suo, nomine *Chochilaicho*, evectu navali per mare Gallias appetunt. Eggressi ad terras pagum unum de regno Theuderici devastant atque captivant, oneratisque navibus tam de captivis quam de reliquis spoliis reverti ad patriam cupiunt. Sed rex eorum in litus residebat, donec naves altum mare comprehenderent, ipse deinceps secuturus. Quod cum Theuderico nunciatum fuisset, Theudebertum, filium suum, in illas partes cum magno exercitu ac magno armorum apparatu direxit. Qui, interfecto rege, hostes navali prœlio superatos opprimit, omnemque rapinam terræ restituit." — *Gregorius Turonensis*, 'Historia Ecclesiastica Francorum,' iii. 3.

An anonymous historian, above seventy years afterwards, whose work is, to a great extent, a reproduction of Gregory's, repeats the account, with an important

---

[2] The credit of identifying Hygelac with Cochilaigus belongs to Outzen, in his paper "Ueber das Angelsächsische Beowulfs Gedicht," in the 'Kieler Blätter' (1816?).—*Thorpe, Translation of 'Beowulf,'* Preface, xxv.

addition, for he tells us that the action took place in the district of the Attuarii.

"In illo tempore Dani cum rege suo, nomine *Cochilago*, cum navale hoste per altum mare Gallias appetunt, Theuderico pagum *Attoarius* et alios devastantes atque captivantes plenas naves de captivis habentes, alto mare intrantes, rex eorum ad litus maris resedit. Quod cum Theuderico nunciatum fuisset, Theudebertum, filium suum, cum magno excercitu in illis partibus dirigens, qui, consequens eos, pugnavit cum eis cæde maxima, atque ipsis prostratis, regem eorum interfecit, prædam tulit et in terram suam restituit."—*Gesta Rerum Francorum*, cxix.

Theudebert was the son of Diedrich (Thierry), the son of Clovis. He was the king of Austrasian Franks, and the date of the descent is A.D. 515 or 516.

A notice that merely tells us that a pirate, who was a Dane, was in a certain year killed in a certain part of the Netherlands, tells us little enough; and, in some respects, tells us worse than nothing, inasmuch as, from the simple impossibility of contradiction, it enables the speculator to take any action of any hero of the same or a similar name, and to connect or identify the two. To a man who is merely known to have died A.D. 516, any exploit within fifty years anterior to that date, and within a limited though somewhat wide range of circumstances, may be attributed. All that can be said, on the first view, as an abatement of this objection, is that the name is a scarce one. It is not one like Olaf, or Harold, or Knut, and a host of others. There is but one Chochilaicus in actual history.

A little more can be got by supposing that, though but one of his deeds (and that the last) is recorded, he may have been, like the brave men who lived before Agamemnon, a hero of much prowess, and of great, though forgotten, renown. And such seems to have been the case. There was a legend in one of the islands of the mouth of the Rhine, that *Hiuglauc*, the king of the *Geats*, was a man of such gigantic stature that, when he was but twelve years of age, no horse could carry him; in proof of which were his bones, which are still to be seen in the island under notice. It would be well if the geologist, by the aid of the tradition, if it still exist, would ascertain the exact locality of the gigantic fossil—saurian or mammalian, as the case may be—which is thus identified with the great sea-king of the sixth century. As for the legend itself, we know with what it is connected, viz. the similar story as to the size of Rolf Ganger, or Rodolf, Raoul, Rollo or Rou, The *Walker*. From its simplicity, and from the slightness in the alteration of the name, this, the Rhenish legend, may pass for the oldest of the notices of Chochilaicus; and, if it be still current, for the one that lasted the longest. In this the great hero is a *Geat*, a term to which we shall soon make a second allusion.

Thirdly, the date of his death was a peculiar one. It belongs to that pre-eminently obscure period between the evacuation of Britain by the Romans and the introduction of Christianity into England under the Frank missionaries. How utterly destitute this era is for definite data in the history of Scandinavia need only be hinted at. That it was but little better in England is best known to those who have examined critically the evidence of what is called the

Anglo-Saxon Conquest, concerning the Ellas, the Cerdics, the Idas, the Stufs, the Wihtgars, the Ceawlins, *et hoc genus omne*, who founded such and such kingdoms in such and such years. Saving the Franks, there are no Germans who can show for this century such a date as that of the death of Chochilaicus; and this is from a Frank writer in Latin. Never, however, was there a period during which a hero, who is known only through his death in the Netherlands, was more likely to have done something, during the days of his activity, on the other side of the German Ocean, than the year A.D. 615. Neither is there any era during which the record of it was more likely to have been lost; or, if not wholly lost, to have been converted into a matter of inference. This means that Chochilaicus was sufficiently a man of note to justify us in associating with his personal history such names as come within probable conditions, and if any such associations connect him with England, they favour rather than impugn the identification.

Fourthly, and this, though it rests on negative evidence, has been long recognized, comes the fact that, whatever it may be in other respects, Chochilaicus is the first name in Danish[3] history, and it is part of the present treatise to show that upon this much depends.

[4] "Der Angriff auf den Gau der Hattuarien um das Jahr 515, aus dem sie von Theodebert, Theoderichs Sohn, mit Verlust ihres Anführers zurückgetrieben wurden, ist der erste Däneneinfall, dessen die fränkischen Annalisten gedenken."—*Zeuss, Die Deutschen und die Nachbarstämme*, pp. 508–9.

A notice of a collision between the Danes and the Heruli is a few years earlier than this defeat of Chochilaicus. In the notice, however, of this event there are no names of any of the individual agents.

Having thus shown a reason for giving the Hugletus of Saxo a predominance over even Vikletus, Vermundus, and Uffo, we now look to his place both in real history and in Saxo's list of kings. In this he is the nineteenth. Three only, (or at most but four, Guthorm, Frotho I., Halfdan, and Rolvo (the sixth, seventh, eighth, and twelfth) bear historical names; but they seem to be names out of their proper place *i.e.* antedated.

The second, Dan I., is an eponymus.

The first, Humble I., is a pro-eponymus, a term, and one upon which more will be said in the sequel.

The third, Humble II., is Humble I. repeated. His co-regent, Lothar, seems to be in the same category with Guthorm, etc.

The fourth is *Skiold*, an eponymus to the dynasty of the *Skioldings*.

The fifth is Gram.

The ninth (the intermediate ones have been already noticed) is Roe, the founder of Roeskilde, much, no doubt, as King Lud of London was the builder of Ludgate.

The tenth and eleventh are Scato and Helgo; the first a divine, the second an heroic name; each mythic rather than historical.

The twelfth is Rolvo, already mentioned.

The thirteenth, Hother, is mythic. In his days Odin and Balder visited Denmark.

The fourteenth, Röric, is merely, so far as the long narrative connected with his reign is concerned, the Amlethus (or rather the Amlethi) of the third and fourth books, though he may be something else besides.

The fifteenth, Viklet, is the successor of Röric, under whom Hamlet's history is continued and brought to a conclusion.

The sixteenth, Vermund, is Uffo's father, Uffo being to Vermund much as Hamlet was to Röric.

The seventeenth, Uffo mysterious and brave as he was during his father's reign, is, after his accession to the throne, no better than Röric. He, doubtless, did great things, but the record is lost. His reign is dispatched in about ten lines, more than half of which are devoted to telling us that there is nothing to be said about it. But more will be said about Uffo hereafter. What, however, we must most especially do with him is this: we must separate Uffo, the son of Vermund, (the Crown Prince, so to say,) from Uffo the King, as decidedly as we are about to separate the Amlethus of the third book from the Amlethus of the fourth.

Then comes Dan II., a repetition of Dan I., the eponymus, he being the eighteenth on the list.

Huglet is the nineteenth, Huglet being, so far as he is Chochilaicus, expressly a *Dane*.

Now what is the difference between *Huglek*, as he will henceforth be called, as the nineteenth king of Denmark in Saxo's list, and *Chochilaicus*, as the bearer of the first name in Danish history? Certainly not the difference between One and Nineteen; for when the two Dans are eliminated as eponymi ; and the two Humbles as pro-eponymi; and Guthorm, Frotho, and Halfdan, as antedated; and the rest of first fourteen as a mixture of myth and inference ; and Röric as a mere lay-figure in the history of Amlethus; and Viklet, Vermund, and Uffo, as

English rather than Danish;—what, I ask, when we have done all this, remains between Huglek and the head of the list? Nothing.

This is our method when we deal with the list as we find it. The place, however, of Huglet in respect to Gormo suggests another explanation. It is with Gormo that the genuine and continuous history of Denmark is considered to begin ; so that both Gormo and Huglek stand at the head of a list. Now the differences in position between these two names is so nearly the difference between those of Huglekus and Humblus, that the probability of Saxo's long serial list being made out of two shorter parallel ones suggests itself, and, as two lists of this kind would consist of twenty names each, these are just the ones every logographer would devise who had been taught to look upon Gorm as the twentieth King of Denmark, counted from either the eponymic Dan or the exceptionally historical Chochilaicus.

That any such calculation was afloat when the two hypothetical lists were first constructed is not known to the present writer by anything like evidence. It is a mere inference from the fact of such relations between two epochs being, whether real or supposed, common in the history of logography, combined with the way in which the present assumption squares with the fact of the two catalogues. In order to bring the two halves into an exact equality some little manipulation is required. The conjoint kings, Humbles II. and Lothar, and Guthorm and Hading may be separated. One of the two Humbles may be omitted. The five kings may be treated as one, and some of the Frothos may be omitted. But, even without this, Dan II.

and Huglekus come very close upon the middle of the
list; and that each of these is just the name with
which a list begins is evident. Dán II., as the head
of one list out of two, is in the place of Dan I., an
eponymus. Huglekus has a similar place as the first
historic Dane. This he is as the representative of
Chochilaicus. Humble, however, is in the same place
as Amlethus in his character of Huglek; while, as
Humble I., he is the father of Dan II. But Dan II.
is the son of Uffo. Uffo, however, is Olaus Mansuetus, who is, again, the Amlethus of the third book.
I do not say that all this gives us even half elements
of the dislocation and confusion here suggested. I
only say that if a succession of equations of this kind
is to be accounted for, it will not be accounted for by
the mere chapter of accidents.

As a point in the credibility of early Danish history
this train of criticism would be important, and much
might be said in its favour. For the present purpose
it is enough for Huglek to be at the head of some
list or other; and this he is according to either of the
views here exhibited.

Place for place, then, and name for name, *Huglek*
and *Chocilaicus*, though not identical, are very near
one another. *Huglek* is the first probable king;
Chochilaicus the first actual historical hero in Denmark. For *Chochilaicus* write *Hygeláo*, and the difference between the names is diminished. And of
both of them this may be predicated,—they are the
names of the first historical Dane who has come down
to us with a name at all.

This is the coincidence which most especially commands our attention. The extent to which Danish

history, after the time of Chochilaicus and Huglek, becomes regular and consecutive is a widely different question, and one to which the answer must be given in the negative. There is certainly a gap between Chochilaicus and the Danes of the eighth century. It is almost as certain that the list of the immediate successors of Huglek is inaccurate. Nevertheless, Frotho II. is more in his proper place than Frotho I.; and so it is with the Halfdans. Indeed, the worst of the names between Huglet and Gorm is in a better predicament than the best of the Dans and Humbles; than Hother, Helgo, Scato, Gram, or Skiold.

Now comes the time for the introduction of a rule which would, if practicable, have been introduced at even an earlier stage of this dissertation. It will be either repeated or alluded to more than once during this work. It will come in at the end, even as it has appeared at the beginning, and is continued throughout; for it is fundamental and essential to the whole line of argument. Yet it is a mere receipt for reading Saxo; or, if we choose our illustration from another quarter, a mere guide-post at the beginning of a journey. We must never, however, either overlook or neglect it.

There is a Third Book and a Fourth Book in Saxo, and between these the reign of the king named Röricus is divided (no other reign being so distributed),—and in the first of these the history of Hamlet begins and in the second ends. Nominally, it is the reign of Röricus; actually, it is the story of Hamlet. Röricus is something less than an Agamemnon. Hamlet is something more than an Achilles. Röricus is next to nowhere; Hamlet is all but every-

C

where. The points, however, to be borne in mind are that there is not one Hamlet, but two; and that the Hamlet of the third book is a different person from the Hamlet of the fourth. This rule is absolute; and, more than this, it is only with the Hamlet of the third book that the Hamlet of Shakespear coincides. The Hamlet of Saxo's third book has little more to do with the Hamlet of the fourth than Shakespear's Hamlet has to do with Shakespear's Macbeth. If there be a fraction of overstatement in this illustration it must be excused. The difference between the two is the difference (to use an old illustration) of Alexander the Great and Alexander the Coppersmith. We shall lose much more by undervaluing than by exaggerating it. There is some connection, some confusion, some action and reaction between them; but in all the essentials, the two Hamlets are, to speak irreverently,—

"Two single gentlemen rolled into one."

Such is the Amlethus, or, rather, the pair of Amlethi of Saxo.

With this pre-eminence given to Hugletus we naturally expect to find that his reign, whether long or short, is treated as one of importance.

The whole history, however, of Huglet as we find it in Saxo is as follows :—

"Post hunc regnat Hugletus, qui Hömothum et Högrimum, Svetiæ tyrannos maritimo fertur oppressisse conflictu." And the notice of it by another writer is equally concise; indeed, it is almost an abridgement of the preceding :—

"Tha var Dan Kunung Uffa sun, ok Huhlek Kunung Uffa sun, han drap tva höfthinga af Suerike, Hemoth ok Hagrim."

This disappoints us. Two lines, along with an unsatisfactory editorial note, is little for the first king of a dynasty and a kingdom, especially when the bearer of the name has been mentioned, with the circumstances of time and place, by the historian of a distant country.

But it is the doctrine of the present writer that no such mutilation of the due proportions of Huglekus really exists. He *has* his history, or what passes for such, and, so far as the mere mass of detail is concerned, it is no smaller than our presumptions make it. How far it is historical is another question.

It is submitted, subject to future argument, that the narrative proper due to *Huglekus* has been transferred to *Amlethus*, and in Saxo's *fourth* book it is to be found under that name. This means that in the fourth book we may read *Huglekus* for *Amlethus*. How this comes to pass is a question which may stand over for a time.

At present it is sufficient to say that the main evidence of the change lies (1) in the results to which it leads, or the harmony or symmetry of the system which arises out of them; and (2) in the ease with which the chief difficulty, the difference between the *words* Huglekus and Amlethus, is surmounted.

In the first place, it converts the trio formed by Viklet, Vermund, and Uffo, into a quaternion, by which the agreement between Saxo and Beowulf is notably increased.

Saxo.	Beowulf.
Huglekus.	Higelac.
Vikletus.	Wiglaf.
Vermundus.	Garmund.
Uffo.	Offa.

From which it follows that so far as the Amlethus of the fourth book is *Huglek* or *Chochilaicus*, he is also *Higelác*, and, *vice versâ*, Higelác is Amlethus. That Higelác and Huglek give Chochilaicus is, it must be, remembered, no new doctrine. The new doctrine, innovation, paradox, suggestion, discovery, interpretation, or whatever it may be called, is that Huglekus is Amlethus. Here, indeed, and no earlier, the present criticism begins. It proceeds by bringing *Havelok*, the Dane, into the same category with *Huglek*, Higelac, and Chochilaicus.

It is only, however, the Amlethus of the *fourth* book who is compared with Huglekus and his parallels, equivalents, or *aliases*.

The Hamlet of the *third* book is Uffo (as *Crown Prince*) who (as *King*) becomes *Olaus Mansuetus*.

But *Olaus Mansuetus* is, *as name*, much the same as Olaus *Tranquillus ;* which is a recognized translation of Olaf *Kyrre;* which is, combination for combination, the Anglo-Saxon *Anlaf Cwiran*, and the Irish *Ambhlaibh Cuaran*. Just, however, as *Olaf* thus fuses with the adjunct *Cuaran*, so does *Havelok*, which comes from Higelác and Chochilaicus. From *Ambhlaibh* it is now submitted that *Amlethus* is an admissible transition. The difficulty, however, of connecting the two names is not supposed to be one between two *words*. It is a confusion between two *individuals*.

So much for the names. How far the details in the way of narrative and evidence support this view must be collected from the sequel. All that need be adduced before we proceed to the *minutiæ* of the question is the notice that it is upon the result, taken as a whole, rather than from the evidence that preseuts itself at each successive step, that the judgment of the reader must be founded.

A writer who professedly makes his investigations on the principle of finding something like an Ariadnean thread to the mysteries of a labyrinth, rather than the topographical details of the maze itself, as after its exploration it could be represented by a map, must tax the reader's patience on two points. He must not be asked to make his exposition interesting by leading him gradually up to unexpected results, and so stimulate his curiosity. The reader must see the plan beforehand. He must look upon the subject as a theorem, rather than a problem. His interest, if he have any in the matter, must be concentrated on the evidence by which it stands or falls, rather than upon any curious result which the inquiry may lead to. But this requires him to tolerate occasional repetitions and occasional anticipations. Of these there shall be as few as possible. Still, there will be some.

Higelac.

Between the death of Cochilaicus and the date of the single known existing manuscript of Beowulf there is an interval of about[*] five hundred years, during which time the name of the Danish sea-king was exposed to all the chances of an imperfect record, —perhaps to those of a mere tradition; and this in three different countries; *i. e.* by inference, in Britain

---

[*] Unfortunately, as of Cædmon and the Codex Exoniensis, there is only a single manuscript of Beowulf extant, which I take to be of the first half of the eleventh century.—*Thorpe, Translation of 'Beowulf,' Preface,* xi.

(which we may now call England), in Denmark, and in the Netherlands. How it survived its bearer in this last country we have seen; for the origin of the tradition is, doubtless, older than the notice of it, and the notice of it is from writers several centuries after the event. The bones that gave rise to it may still exist, —possibly in some well-frequented geological museum, with an able exposition of their real nature, and a Greek name for the extinct animal to which they originally belonged. The title, however, of the traditional proprietor, *Huiglauc*, is genuine.

As far, then, as the outward and visible signs of fame are concerned, the great name of the first of the historical Danes is concealed for four centuries, and when it appears in the poem of Beowulf, it is not that of the hero and protagonist, but that of a secondary personage; secondary, however, only as a hero. In rank he is the superior to Beowulf, and, in a composition especially appropriated to himself, he would, perhaps, be at least his equal in heroism. As it is, he is as Agamemnon to an Achilles, or as Charlemagne to Roland. However, even thus, he is always mentioned as a man of a sufficient note to be alluded to without explanation, or as one of whom an adequate knowledge might be taken for granted. At present, this is as much as need be said. Actual parallelism is not to be expected where in one narrative the name of the person compared is that of a secondary character, in the other, that of a protagonist.

There is another caution to be inculcated. Chochilaicus is a Danish Rink. Higelac is a *Geat*, which may be either *Goth* or *Jute*, the latter being its more natural meaning. But though called a *Geat*, there is much which connects him with Englishmen, for Wærmund, Offa, and Wiglaf, his cotemporaries, are English. The present doctrine which makes him a a *Dane* of *Jutland*, settled in *England*, reconciles these discrepancies,—discrepancies upon which much criticism has been bestowed.

The poem itself, which may almost claim the honourable title of epic, consisting of more than six thousand lines, though written in the short alliterative metre of the Anglo-Saxons, is, when compared with the incidents essential to its structure, a long one. For these are eminently simple. Three fights with three monsters (one of them being against two at once), in the first two of which Beowulf is victorious, but in the last of which he is killed, form the nucleus of it. All beyond is episode and allusion, for which the feasts in celebration of his victories, and other adventitious narratives, supply opportunities. Individually, I think it gives us at least three shorter poems fused into one ; so that the elements are older than the final form. This, while it subtracts from its unity, adds to the antiquity of its subject-matter.

Hrothgar builds a palace named Heorot, of which all that we know for certain is that it stood in the neighbourhood of a fen, perhaps a Danish, perhaps an English one. Here he is seriously plagued by a water-fiend named Grendel. Him Beowulf conquers, and episodes follow. Then he conquers him along with his mother,—the devil and the devil's dam ; and similar episodical allusions succeed. Finally, he is himself killed by a fire-drake. In the last struggle Wiglaf helps him. With this exception all the other characters are but loosely connected with the main action. Higelác, however, has the foremost place among them, though even here he is secondary. But there are two Beowulfs: Beowulf the Scylding, and Beowulf the Wægmunding, the latter being the true hero.

The most special piece of evidence that identifies *Higelác* with *Chochilaicus*, both as word for word, and man for man, is the following:—

> The quarrel was formed,
> Fierce against *the* Hugas,
> After *Hygelac* came,
> Faring with a naval force
> To Friesland ;
> Where him the *Hetwœras*
> In war vanquished.
>   5819–5825.

As *Hetwaras* is *Attoarii*, which is *Chattuarii*, the letter change from *ch* to *h* is verified for both names, and the connection of *Chochilaicus* with the *Chattuarii* is that of *Higelác* with the *Hetwæras*.

So much for the locality. The date of Higelac is that of Hengist; for Hnæf[5] the Hocing, Hrothgar the Dane, Higelac the Geat, and Hengest the Jute, are all vassals under Healfdene. On the other hand, Fin is the king of the Frisians, and Hildeburh is his queen. Hnæf is slain in a murderous battle against him. A truce follows, when the body of Hnæf is burnt. Hengist meditates, and finally takes, his revenge on Fin ; and when Fin is slain, Hildeburh is

---

[5] In Latin this would be *Cneph*, or *Cniva Chaucus*, Hnæf being a true German name. It is from some one of Hnæf's that Hanover has been believed to take its name.

borne off to Denmark. A connection, however, with Hengest cannot be said to prove a connection with England. It merely suggests a presumption of one.

In respect to his genealogy, Higelac is the son of Hrethel; and Herebeald and Hætheyn are his brothers. Thus:—

Hrethel

Herebeald   Hætheyn   Higelac

Of whom Beowulf says :—

> Hrethel, the king,
> Gave we treasure and feasting,
> Of our kinship was mindful,
> I was not to him, in life,
> In aught more welcome,
> A warrior in his burghs
> Than any of his children,
> Herebeald and Hætheyn,
> Or my Higelac.
>
> 4852–4860.

Now, this is not incompatible with the descent of Chochilaicus; for Chochilaicus, like Melchizedek, so far as history is concerned, has neither father nor mother. He may be any one's son, and any one may be credited with his parentage. He may or may not, then, have been the son of Hrethel. I do not, however, imagine that he was so, and I doubt whether Higelac was; or, rather, I treat the consideration of the question as irrelevant. It seems pretty certain that the father of Chochilaicus, *eo nomine* and *totidem literis*, was unknown, and the same may be said in respect to his representative. Higelac's parentage is certainly possible, but it is the only one which is so.

The father of Huglekus is Dan II.; a name which tallies very well with the fact of the bearer's son being the first of the historical Danes, but which is anything but favourable to the notion of his having been a real individual. Of Havelok, the father is Birkabeyn; of Hamlet, Horvendil;—both, for widely different reasons, impossible parents.

With Havelok Higelác agrees in his connection with England; with the Amlethus of the Fourth Book in a similar connection with England, and his superadded relations with Wiglaf, Wærmund, and Offa. Of anything beyond this, in the way of either a connection or dissociated, there are only two pieces of detail which deserve notice.

Of extracts, however, like the following—

When from home had heard
Higelac's thane (*i. e.* Beowulf)
(A good man among the Geats)
Of Grendel's deeds;
Who of mankind was
In power strongest
In that day
Of this life
Noble and vigorous
He bade for him a wave-traverser
Good be prepared.
390–400.

there are perhaps as many as twenty. They are all, however, to the same purpose; all general and indefinite; all limited to the statement, slightly changed according to the circumstance, of the relation between Higelác and Beowulf being that of lord and thane. The two that are sufficiently special to command a fuller exposition relate to Higelác,—

1. As the possessor of the Brosinga-mén;
2. As the husband of Hygd.

This is to be compared with Hamlet's Shield; Hamlet being, of course, the Amlethus of Saxo's

Fourth Book. Such, too, is also the case with the second extracts. Higelac and the Amlethus of Book III. are wholly incommensurable.

(1.)

The Brosinga-men.

Thorpe's Translation.

To him the cup was borne,
and friendly invitation
in word offer'd,
and twisted gold
kindly shown,
sleeves two,
a mantle and rings,
of collars the largest
of those that I on earth
have heard tell of:
not any under heaven I
more excellent have heard of
treasure-hoard of men,
since Hama bore off
to the noble bright city
the Brosings' necklace,
the jewel and its casket:
he into the guileful enmity
    fell
of Eormenric;
and chose th' eternal council.
That ring had
Hygelac the Goth,
Swerting's nephew,

the last time
when he under his banner
his treasure defended,
guarded the spoil of the
    slain:
him fate took off,
after he for pride
sought his own woe,
a war with the Frisians:
he the ornament convey'd,
the precious stones,
over the cup of waves,
the powerful king;
he fell beneath his shield:
departed then into the grasp
    of the Franks
the king's life,
his breast-weeds,
and the collar also:
worse warriors
plunder'd the fall'n,
after the lot of war;
the Goths' people
held the mansion of the dead.

2390—2432.

2.

The Lady Hygd.

She is to be compared with Hamlet's bad wife.

Thorpe's Translation.

The mansion was excellent,
a chief renown'd the king;
high *the* hall;
Hygd very young,
wise, well-nurtur'd,
though winters few
amid *the* burgh-enclosure
had abided
Hæreth's daughter;
although she was not mean,
nor of gifts too sparing
to *the* Goths' people,
of treasure-acquisitions,
yet violence of mood mov'd
the folks' bold queen,
crime appalling.
No one durst that
beast address,
of *the* dear companions,
save her wedded lord,
who on her daily
with eyes gazed;
but to him a death-band
decreed, calculated,
hand-bound,
was quickly after,
after *the* hand-grasp,
with *the* sword resolv'd,
so that the pernicious brand
must decide,
the deadly bale make known;
such is no feminine usage
for a woman to practise,
although she be beautiful,
that a peace-weaver
machinate *to deprive* of life

after burning anger
a dear man;
at least with that reproached
　her
Heming's son,
while drinking ale;
Others said,
that she dire evils
less perpetrated,
direful iniquities,
after *she* was first,
given gold-adorned,
to *the* young warrior,
the noble beast,
after she Offa's court,
over *the* fallow flood,
through *her* father's counsel,
by journey sought,
where she afterwards well,
on *the* throne,
the good and great
life's creations
living enjoy'd,
high love entertained
towards the prince of heroes,
of all mankind,
as I have heard
the best
between the seas,
of the human race;
for Offa was,
for gifts and wars
(*a* bold man in arms)
widely honour'd;
he in wisdom held
his country;

from him[6] Eomer sprang Garmund's grandson
for help to heroes   mighty in conflict.
Heming's son

ll. 3929.

"The preceding digression about Hygd and Offa," remarks Mr. Thorpe in a note, "is barely intelligible." It points, however, to some dark traits in Hygd's character. After Higelác's death, she first offers her hand to Beowulf, who refuses it. That she marries Offa we have just seen. So mysterious, however, are her conjugal relations, that, though Thorpe makes her Higelác's wife, Kemble can scarcely say whether she is Higelác's or Offa's. However, Higelác is now dead, slain in Friesland.

Nor was that least
of hand-meetings,
where Hygelac was slain,
when *the* Goths' king.
In war onslaughts,
the lordly friend of nations,
In the Frieslands,
Hrethel's offspring,
Sword-drunken perished,
By *the* falchion beaten.
Thence Beowulf came
By *his* own power,
The need of swimming suffer'd;
He had on his arm
. . . . . thirty
War-equipments.
When he to *the* sea went down.
Not *the* Hetwæras
Had need of exultation
In that host of war,

Who in front against him
Bore the linden;
Few again came
From that warlike darer,
Their home to visit;
Swam over the seal's course
Ecgtheow's son (*i. e.* Beowulf),
a poor solitary,
Again to his people,
Where him Hygd offer'd
Treasure and realm,
Rings and princely throne:
In her child she trusted not,
That he against foreign folks
His paternal seats
Could hold.
Then was Hygelac dead,
Yet not for that sooner *the*
poor *people*
Could prevail

[6] Compare *Eumer* suborned by Curchelm to stab Edwin, King of Northumberland.

with the prince
on any account,
That he to Heardred (Hyge-
    lac's son)
would be Lord,
or the kingdom
would choose ;

Yet he him among *his* people
With friendly instructions
    maintain'd
Kindly with honour ;
Until he became older
And ruled the Weder-Goths.

ll. 4747.

The Brosinga-mén and Hygd have been noticed thus fully, not so much because they are the two special details connected with the name of Higelác, but because they will both be met with again.

HAVELOK THE DANE.

The interval between the recognized date of Beowulf and the earliest notice of Havelok the Dane is about[7] two hundred years, and very important ones they are; since, upon the connection between Havelok with Higelác or Chochilaicus, who goes before, and Amlethus, who follows after him, nine-tenths of the present treatise depends.

Havelok stands like Janus, looking both ways. We must consider him as the bearer of a name, and we must consider the story connected with him. It is in the latter respect that he differs most notably from Higelác and Chochilaicus. In Beowulf Higelác is only a secondary character ; in the romance that bears his name Havelok is all-in-all, and we may add that the two poems are of a widely different character. As for Chochilaicus it has already been stated that all we know of him is that he lived and died; and that in probably three countries he left his mark behind him ; beyond this, however, he is merely

[7] See note p. 21.

the owner of a name round which attributes and narratives, generally heterogeneous, and almost always foreign to the historical individual, as round some organic nucleus, have gravitated and accumulated; and that to such a degree that the original Chochilaicus, if not wholly transmuted, ends in being the least part of himself. Sometimes we are fortunate enough to trace these accretions to their own proper sources; in which case we get, by the method of exclusion, some approximation to the real personality of the central or fundamental figure. With this we must generally be content. I think that with Havelok and Chochilaicus we can, certainly, do thus much, and I fear we can do no more.

Chochilaicus, Hiuglauc, Higelac, and Havelok are the same names; and, so far as the bearer of them was a single hero, the three are one. In the supposed bones of the giant of the Netherlands, the historical sea-king undoubtedly left his mark on the Lower Rhine; and he is further supposed to have left them in Britain in the stories of Higelac and Havelok. As a Dane, then, on English ground, and as a king or captain of note, we may make a guess about Chochilaicus; but further than this we may not profess to do anything. All beyond is the history of certain foreign additions which his fame has brought within the sphere of its attraction.

This we must clearly understand; for it is on one point only that the comparison of *Havelok* with *Higelac* is clear enough to speak for itself, or to stand on its own merits, independent of *primâ facie* objections. This point is the name. Word for word, *Havelok* is merely the Danish form of *Higelac*, and

Higelác, the Anglo-Saxon of *Havelok*. In the details, however, of the two narratives there is no such likeness. Indeed there is, to some extent, a contrast. Whether this has prevented the connection between the poem of Beowulf, so far as it relates to Higelac and the Havelok romances being recognized, is more than I can say. It may have done so or it may not. I could certainly, for the sake of the present argument, have wished that the relation here suggested had, by having been recognized by some of my predecessors, come down to me as an admitted fact, and that the identity of Havelok and Higelac stood in the same category with that of Higelac and Chochilaicus. On the other hand it must be remembered that it was not until the eleventh hour that the two poems on Havelok were known to the public. Outzen knew nothing about them; and though the two texts were published during the days of both Kemble and Thorpe, they were not published until each of those scholars had gone far enough in his study of Beowulf to have formed an opinion independent of them. Such, in my mind, is the true explanation of their silence; at any rate I should be sorry to think that the comparison of Havelok and Higelac was one which they had condemned rather than overlooked. The importance of the double connection here claimed for Havelok is beyond doubt. He is more like Higelac in name than in deed. He is more like Amlethus in deed than in name.

But what if there are two claimants to the very name, and two claimants to the actions connected with it? Such is the case. If it were not so, our task would be easy; for it would merely consist in

the elimination of the manifestly adventitious elements from the stories of the French and English
Havelok; the result being that Havelok, like Higelac and Chochilaicus, was a Danish king or captain
who left his mark in England during the sixth cen-
century, etc., as has just been stated. But, even
when this is obtained, we are unfortunately in the
dark, inasmuch as we are not sure of his relation to
the history of either England or Denmark, inasmuch
as there is a second historical hero of whom both
Danish blood and English notoriety may be predicated; and, what is more perplexing still, he bears a
name which might pass into that of *Havelok*.

It has long been known that the name of Havelok
appears in the story of the famous Guy, Earl of
Warwick, who, by killing the Norwegian giant Col-
brand, freed Northumberland from its allegiance to
the Danes, to which it had been subject since the
time of Hanelocke. It is hard to believe that this *n*
is not properly a *v*; indeed the substitution may be a
mere clerical error. The passage runs thus:—

"Athelstone lay at Winchestre, and the king of Denmark sent ynto him an harowde of armes, to witte, whether
he wold fynde a man to fight with Colbrande for the right
of the kyngdom of Northumbr, that the Danes had claimed
before by the title of Kyng *Haneloke*, that wedded Goldesburge, the king's daughter of Northumbr."

As however it was Havelok who married Goldes-
burg, it is Havelok who is here indicated. Only,
however, in this special extract. In the following,
though the spelling is the same, and the event alluded to the same, Hanelok is a different person,
and, what is more, a real historical one.

D

> "But or Guy went that man him tolde,
> That the King was in cases colde,
> The King of Denmarke, *Hanelocke*,
> And the King of Norway, *Conelocke*."

Here Hanelocke is the associate of Conelocke, who is an Irishman of the tenth century.

"An. DCCCCXLIV. Blacar expulsus e Dublinio, et *Amlaf* ei succedit. Pars gentis O'Cannanorum occisa per *Congalac*, et *Amlaf Cuaran* in Conallia."—*Annales Uttonienses*.

The same names, with the same spelling, appear again in 946–7. In the Irish, of which the Latin is a translation, *Amlaf* is spelt *Amlaip*. Anelaphus is also an English form.

Bodl. Laud. 636.	*Cott. Dom. A.* VIII.
An. DCCCC . XLIX. Her com Anlaf *Cwiran* on Norð hymbraland.	An. DCCCC. XLIX. Her com Anlaf *Cwiran* on Norðhymbraland.
An. DCCCC.L., DCCCC.LI.	An. DCCCC.L., DCCCC.LI.
An. DCCCC.LII. Her Norð-hymbre fordrifan Anlaf cyning, and underfongon [8]Yric Haroldes sunu.	An. DCCCC.LII. Her Norð-hymbre fordriuon Anelaf cing . and underfengon Yric Haroldes sunu.

The reason why the particular MSS. give the adjunct *Cwiran* will soon become evident. There is confusion here, but it does not affect the important word under notice.[9] There is confusion, but we can see our way through it. There are two series of names which were originally different, but which here become confluent, or rather, proceeding from opposite points meet and mix midway; not without

---

[8] *Eric* is the name of the usurping uncle in the Dramatis Personæ of the *German* " Hamlet " and Warner's tale of " Argentile and Curan."

[9] Sax. Chron.

antagonism. Thus on one side we have Chochilaicus, Higelac, and Havelok ; on the other, Olaus, Olaf, and Anlaf ; whilst at the point of contact between the two lines we get, applied to the same person, Hane-lock, which points to Havelok, and Anelaph, which suggests Anlaf. Which is *our* hero ? Both or neither. It is this very confusion or ambiguity which helps to the mystery of his personality.

It must not seem strange that notwithstanding all the associations which connect Hamlet, Prince of Denmark and a Scandinavian, along with the reasons here given for identifying *Havelok the Dane* with *Chocilaicus* the result should be that, of all countries in the world, Ireland is the one to which the Amlethus of Saxo must be directly referred. That some such form as *Amlaf* is needed to account for the change of name is simply part and parcel of the present line of criticism, and so is the doctrine that Ireland is the country which supplies it. But it may naturally be argued by those to whom Ireland seems an impossible source, that such a necessity, by proving too much, invalidates the whole train of reasoning. Be it so. But is Ireland in reality thus impossible ? Is it even improbable ? Is it not rather one of the first countries towards which we look ? Next to Great Britain and Germany, and perhaps Finland, Ireland was the country which the Scandinavians looked upon with the most interest. When Iceland was discovered, and it was a question whether it had ever before been trodden by the foot of man, the possibly prior population was referred to Ireland. The holy island of Iona, Irish in language, though Scotch in geography, was as much Norwegian as Irish. The important work upon history, geography, and history, written *exceptionally* in the Old Norse of Norway rather than in that of Iceland, the 'Mirrour of Kings,' gives more space to what then passed for the topography, the geography, and the history of Ireland than to all the other descriptions of all the other parts of the world put together. Thirdly, the Irish Annals give us not less than four different *Amlafs* as kings either of Ireland or of certain parts of it. The date of Amlaf Cuaran is A.D. 950. The Amlaf who was defeated at Brunanburg was just dead. Then, assigned to A.D. 850, or a full century earlier, we[10] find Amelaus, or Amelavus, as king of Dublin, with two other of his countrymen and brothers ruling contemporaneously in Limeric and Waterford. Finally, whatever may be the difficulty in determining the origin of the story of Saxo's Amlethus, it is the unanimous opinion of the commentators that it is not to be found in Scandinavia. No such name occurs in any Icelandic record; for, though there exists a Hamlet's Saga, it is acknowledged to be founded on Saxo's narrative, —the source of Saxo's narrative being as uncertain as ever.

After an anticipation of objections like this it seems useless to add that, after all, it is not in Ireland that we must look for the *original* source. *Olaf*, the son of Sihtric, began, as a historical king, either in Scandinavia or as a Scandinavian. His name in England took the form of *Anlaf*. In Ireland it became *Amhlaf*. It reached—probably through the Orkneys and Norway—Denmark in

---

[10] Only, however, in the later writers.

a form which in Latin became *Amlethus;* and,
as it had passed through the English and Irish
languages before, it is no wonder that it was not
recognized on its return to its native country. It
had been so altered during its passage through two
languages as to look like a stranger. Still less was
it like *Hugleik,* or *Hugletus.* In fact, then, Amlethus
is English after the fashion of Vermundus, Vikletus,
and Uffo; but changed, in both form and import,
from having passed through Ireland. The history of
the two countries fully sustains this hypothesis.

Thus far the association of Henelok with Congalac
on the one side, and with Goldsburgh on the other,
has been our only evidence in favour of names so unlike as Olaus and Chochilaicus taking the *same* form.
It can now be improved; and that by attending to the
import of the word *Cuaran* or *Cwiran,* which has
already presented itself twice; in the 'Ulster Annals'
and in the 'Anglo-Saxon Chronicle.' The date, however, of the events with which it is connected is one
thing, the entry of the name itself another. The
latter may much later than the former.

Now Anlaf Cwiran and Amblabh Cuaran point
beyond doubt to Olaf the son of Sihtric. The Cuaran of the following continuation points as undoubtedly to Havelok the Dane.

> *Haveloc* fut cit roi nomé
> Et *Cuaran* est appellée.
> Pour ces vus voit de lui conter
> Et s'aventure remembrer;
> Q'un lai en firent li Breton,
> Et l'appellèrent de son non
> Et Haveloc et *Cuarant.*
>
> *Gaimar,* ll. 17–23.

The following passage, from the same poem, more important still, gives us the reason he was so called, or the origin of the word *Cuaran.* It is one, however, which has never been confirmed, and one that merely represents the fancy of either the writer or some of his authorities. The Danish is the language in which, ere long, we shall discover its import. At present, however, let us note the contents of the extract. Havelok is a hewer of wood, a drawer of water, and a washer of dishes; a strong churl nevertheless, and liberal to his fellow-servants. Whenever a piece of bread or a slice of meat might be welcome to them, he gave it them willingly. Indeed, his excess of liberality, easiness of temper, and the pleasure he took in serving others, made him pass for something like a fool. So they called him Cuaran, which in the Breton language means *Quistron.*

> Merveillous fés poeit lever,
> Busche taiiler, ewe porter.
> Les esquielles recevoit
> Et après manger les lavoit;
> Et quant-qu'il poeit purchacer,
> Pièce de char ou pain enter,
> Mult le donait volentiers
> As valets et as esquiers.
> Tant estoit franc et deboneire,
> Qe tuz voloit lur pleisir fere.
> Pur la franchise qe il ont
> Entre eux le tenoient pur sot;
> De lui fesoient lur deduit,
> *Cuaran* l'appelloient tuit;
> Car ceo tenoient li Breton
> En lur language *quistron.*

> *Ibid.,* ll. 244–360.

It is Gaimar's Chronicle from which these extracts are taken. Passages, however, with a similar impoit occur in the French version of the Romance,—in the French, but not in the English. With this limitation, however, the evidence of the fusion is amply adequate. This is what we find in the twelfth century. Just before the end of the sixteenth, Warner, one of the minor poets of the Elizabethan period, published his long and once popular poem, entitled 'Albion's England,' in which the tale of Argentile and Curan forms a well-known episode. It is founded on the story of Havelok the Dane. It is, too, either founded on the Romance or the same version of the story. At any rate, the name of the heroine is Argentile, and not, as in the English, Goldsborough; and the name of the hero is *Curan*, not Havelok,—not Havelok *Curan*, but *Curan* purely and simply.

Such is the evidence of the confusion between Havelok and Anlaf; no matter how it may be accounted for, or, indeed, whether it can be accounted for at all. It is a confusion between Havelok and Anlaf as man and man; not between "*Havelok*" and "*Hamlet*" as word and word. It is a mixture of personalities; not a matter of letter-changes. The husband of Goldsburgh and the Cuaran of Warner's poem are one individual; the associate of Conelok in Ireland is another.

It is in this stage, then, of the development of our legend to which the important change of name is to be referred; and we shall find that it does not stand alone. We now, for the first time, find elements which indicate the Hamlet of Saxo's *Third* Book.

Such is his connection with the kitchen. Warner
calls Curan a "scullion" *totidem literis.* It is to the
kitchen that Saxo's Hamlet is banished by his uncle.
It is the kitchen and the cellar which one of his bio-
graphers makes the chief resorts of Uffo.[11] Like
Hamlet, too, and Uffo, Havelok Cuaran passes for
anything but a wise man; though, as his story proceeds, he undeceives the world upon this point. This
is what is done by both Uffo and Hamlet. Lastly,
we have already seen that Uffo was also called Olaus
Mansuetus, and we shall soon see that of *Olaus Mansuetus Anlaf Cuaran* (or *Amblaibh Cuaran*) is something more than a legitimate translation.

THE AMLETHUS OF SAXO'S THIRD BOOK.

Gorvendil, Hamlet's grandfather, has two sons,—
Horvendil, Hamlet's father, and Fengo, the murderous brother and the usurping uncle.

The members of the Hamlet family are not royal,
but hold territory in either Sleswick or Jutland,
under Röric, the true king of Denmark, whose capital is at Leire.

Röric has a daughter named Grytha, whom he
gives in marriage to Horvendil, and she is Hamlet's
mother. He has also a son, Vikletus, to whom
Hamlet (in the Fourth Book) acts much as Fengo
had acted towards himself, as a usurping *nephew.*
This *maternal* uncle of Hamlet plays an important
part in the history of Hamlet when we read it in
full.

---

[11] "Nam ab infantia præfatus Uffo ventris indulgebat ingluvici, et,
Epicurorum more, *coquinæ* et cellario alternum officiose impendebat."
—*Historia Regum Daneæ,* ch. 1.

Horvendil had won the hand of Grytha by his victories over the famous Norwegian viking Kollar and his sister Sela, also over the Slaves and Courlanders.

As soon as an opportunity presented itself, Fengo murdered his brother; for, "perceiving himself strong enough to execute his enterprise, Horvendill, his brother, being at a banquet with his friends, [he] sodainely set upon him, whene he slew him as traitorously, as cunningly he purged himself of so detestable a murther to his subjects; for that before he had any violent or bloody handes, or once committed parricide upon his brother, he had incestuously abused his wife, whose honour hee ought as well to have sought and procured as traiterously he pursued and effected his destruction." There was, then, no mystery about Horvendil's murder, so that no ghost was needed to reveal it.

The persecution of the son coincided with the marriage of the mother; and with these began the simulated madness.

Hamlet, after his father's death and his mother's marriage, instead of being treated with insincere kindness, is, from the first, degraded and humiliated. He is banished to the kitchen, and, by the kitchen fire, he makes playthings of bits of wood. These he cuts or whittles into barbed skewers and hooks, and when asked what they are meant for, replies, "to revenge my father's murder." He passes for either an idiot or a lunatic, but there is always method in his madness. It is thoroughly fictitious. The only sign of folly that Hamlet shows is his extreme candour. He makes no secret of what he means. It is no easy matter, however, to sustain a double import throughout a series of sayings and doings; nor are Saxo's examples of the happiest. Sometimes he gives us a piece of practical buffoonery, as when Hamlet rides a horse with his head towards the animal's tail. One speech, perhaps, "darkens to sublimity," for he says of a ship's rudder that "it is a knife for a big hog,"—the ocean. But of images like these the old Scandinavian poetry is full, and over-full.

The details of Hamlet's temptation differ. The novel gives the fewest of them. Here Hamlet is "viciously provoked" by a gentlewoman, he being previously conducted by a set of courtiers to a solitary place within the woods. Of these one was his foster-brother (collactaneus), who "by certain signes" gives Hamlet "intelligence to what danger he was likely if by any meanes he seemed to obaye, or once like the wanton and vicious provocations of a gentlewoman sent thither by his uncle." This abashed the prince, for he loved the lady, and the lady loved him; they having also been foster-children, — "uterque eosdem infantes procuratores habuerit. Domum itaque reductus, cunctis an Veneri indulgisset, per ludibrum interrogantibus puellam a se construpratam fætetur. Puella de ea re interrogata nihil eum tale gessisse perhibuit." There is a good deal of cross-questioning, and not a little *equivoque* in the examination of this matter. Neither the questions, however, nor the answers are worth giving.

The "certain signes" by which the friend of Hamlet contrived to inform him that he was watched gives us a riddle which certainly required a wise man to rede. It taxed the ingenuity of Hamlet, and it has certainly perplexed the commentators. The prince's monitor, however, catches a horsefly, gadfly, or waterfly (*œstrus*), and impaling it with a straw sets its free. How it was to find its way to the bower of Hamlet and his gentlewoman we know not. However, it reaches them; and when Hamlet sees it, takes warning accordingly. How Hamlet read the riddle we are not informed. Müller reads it is a sign that, inasmuch as insects are not given to impale themselves, human beings must be in the neighbourhood:—

"Considerans enim, quonam aptuis modo occultum monitoris officium exequi periculosamque juvenis lasciviam præcurrere posset, repertam humi paleam œstri prætervolantis caudæ submittendum curavit. Eget deinde ipsum in ea potissimum loca, quibus Amlethum in esse cognovit; eoque facto maximum incanto beneficium attulit. Nec callidius transmissum indicium, quam cognitum fuit. Siquidem Amlethus, viso œstro simulque stramine, quod caudæ insitum gestabat, curiosius per notato, tacitum cavendæ fraudis monitum intellexit."

It is possible that in the following passage this *œstrus* may be reproduced, *Osric* being the *man of the waterfly*, or the friend who served Hamlet under his temptation, as opposed to Horatio, who seems to have nothing to do with it, answers to which, "in the decent obscurity of a learned language," we have alluded, it is decided that Hamlet must be mad; yet, at the same time, in the opinion of his uncle at least, dangerous.

Then follows the interview with his mother, and the killing of Polonius,—the spied spy. Hamlet

enters, crowing and flapping his arms like a cock ;
then, suspecting an eaves-dropper, and whipping out
his sword kills the prying counsellor through the
arras.   But he does not as Shakespear, and even in
Belleforest cry "a rat, a rat."   For the rest, however,
of the scene the translator and original agree, and
when we learn that in so doing they tell us how the
dead body is cut up, boiled, and given to the hogs,
not to mention other details equally nauseous, we
are glad that the dramatist has ignored their narrative.

The voyage to England now suggests itself; for
Fengo is still both supicious and fearful; fearful of
the queen and her father.   So bethinking himself of
a king of England (his name is unknown), he sends
Hamlet to him with letters.   The letters, which the
bearer opens during the voyage, are to the effect that
Hamlet shall be put to death; upon reading which,
they are altered accordingly.   What then the king
of England reads is as follows—that the two companions and conductors of Hamlet's voyage are to be
executed, and that Hamlet himself is to be married
to the king's daughter.

Now, on leaving Denmark, Hamlet, who had
visited his mother, had privily prevailed upon her to
undertake to cover the walls of a chamber with
tapestry, held up by means of loops and pullies, and,
at the end of a year to enact a false funeral service
over himself as if dead.   While this was doing he
would present himself alive.

We may now ask how he fared in England.   One
of Saxo's doctrines is, that there was not only in
Hamlet's equivocal answers a great deal of wisdom,

but that his whole conduct, notwithstanding appearances to the contrary, was characterized by the strictest adherence to the truth. Whatever may have been the case in Denmark, his conscientiousness deserts him as he approaches England. His companions present the letters, altered as they have been to their own disadvantage, but the king dissimulates, and invites them to a feast. Nothing, however, will Hamlet touch; so that as far as he is concerned the banquet is taken off untasted. As this excites wonder, a spy is set upon Hamlet to hear what he and his friends say when, before retiring for the night, they talk over the events of the day; the leading topic being Hamlet's strange behaviour at the feast.

" Why, when abstinence was an insult to his host, would he neither eat nor drink ?"

" How should I," said the prince, " when the bread was bloody, and the drink smacked of iron, and the meat had the taste of man's flesh ? The king, too, has the visage of a slave, while the queen thrice comported herself like a serving-maid."

There was no doubt now about his madness; only, however, among his immediate hearers. The king, on the contrary, opined that the man who spoke thus was quite as likely to be a sage as a simpleton, " Supra mortalium habitum aut sapere aut desipere." So the steward is examined about the bread, when he owns that the field in which the corn was grown had been manured with human bones from a neighbouring battle-field. The meat? The pigs had battened on the rotten carcase of a robber. The drink (hydromel)? Some rusty swords were found in the water, and the bees that made the honey (as in Sampson's honeycomb) had been bred in a carrion.

But, if these answers satisfied the king as to the soundness of Hamlet's understauding, they disturbed him as to the question of his own legitimacy. What if the charge against himself of being the son of a slave were as valid as the exceptions taken to the viands? His mother, however, when cross-questioued, owned that she had disgraced herself. The only problem now standing over was the alleged vulgarity of the queen. What were the three points that betrayed her? Hamlet alone can answer this. The first was that she covered her head with a cloak.

" Free women," says the commentator, " wore caps which servants did not; so that the latter, when they went out in the air, pulled their cloaks over their heads."

The second was, that she wore her gown tucked-up. The third that she picked her teeth during her meals. Of a son-in-law with wisdom like this any monarch might be proud. So his daughter is betrothed to Hamlet at once, and within four-and-twenty hours the two attendants are hanged. And here disappears, to everyone but the over-partial Saxo, the last trace of our hero's vaunted truthfulness. Nothing is more agreeable to Hamlet than the execution. Yet he affects disapproval, and clothes himself with virtuous indignation. He puts also, as the price of his forgiveness, a large sum of gold. This he melts down, and encases in the hollow of two truncheons; with which, and after passing them off as ordinary staves of wood, he leaves England for Denmark in the twelfth month of his visit, according to the previous

arrangement with his mother. Denmark he reaches
on the anniversary of his departure. His mother
had declared him dead, so that, in fact, he came as a
mourner at his own funeral. We shall now do well
to remember his instructions about the hangings,
texilibus nodis, also about the skewers and daggers,
with which we cut and carved in the days when he
lived in the kitchen, and, connected with which there
was a prophetic explanation of their import.

Now, however, he meets the funeral procession as
a man alive, and is put upon the bier like a corpse;
squalid in his garb, rambling in his talk. Some of
the followers look serious; more, however, fall to
gibing and jesting. " Where are your mates— those
that went to England with you ?"

"Here," says Hamlet, holding out his two truncheons
with their cores of gold. " Now this," writes Saxo,
still stickling for the latent veraciousness of all his
hero's sayings and doings was " both a good jest and
a good truth, for what was the gold which the
truncheons enclosed but the compensation-money for
their deaths, and, as such, their equivalents ?" The
feast begins, and Hamlet mixes with the waiters,
careful that no one shall want drink; but, in order
that he may move more freely, he girds his sword on
his side, taking care to be continually pulling it out;
yet, at the same time, handling it so unskilfully that
he cuts his fingers. To stop this, the attendants nail
the blade to the sheath. Meanwhile the drinking
increases, and all become drunk. The time for
Hamlet's old machinations having arrived, the hangings with the knots are let down upon the staggering
and sleeping carousers, and the hooks and skewers

that had been charred in the kitchen-fire, are fixed
in them as pegs.   In short, when the whole company is covered, as by a big casting-net, a torch is
applied, and the whole crew, with the single exception
of the usurping uncle, burnt to death.

For him another fate is reserved.   He had gone
to bed before the drinking had reached its height,
with his sword by his side on the bed.   This Hamlet
takes to himself, leaving his own, which, from having
its blade and sheath nailed together, was useless in
its place.   We anticipate the result, especially when
we call to mind the change of foils between Laertes
and Hamlet in the closing scene of the play.   Fengo
is awakened, and hears from Hamlet the fate of his
courtiers.   He hears, too, what use has been made of
the hooks and skewers; and, lastly, that the hour has
at length come when the murderer of Horvendil is
to meet his just punishment.   He grasps his sword,
which is, of course, as useless as a broken reed; so
that his nephew kills him without either difficulty or
remorse.

THE AMLETHUS OF SAXO'S FOURTH BOOK.

With the death of Fengo, the fratricide, the *third*
book of Saxo ends; and, if the parallel between the
Shakesperian and the Saxonian Hamlets ran on all-
fours, the history of Hamlet would end also.   What,
however, we actually find in Saxo is the very reverse
of this; indeed the Hamlet of the *fourth* book is the
reverse of his former self.   We may *almost* say that
the heroes of the two books are two different individuals, so slight is the connection between them.

The Hamlet of the fourth book is no weakling in any sense of the word, neither is he either fool or idiot, natural or pretending.   On the contrary, he is a warrior of the true Norse type, and a politician and strategist of unrivalled cunning.   It cannot, however, be denied that, different as the Hamlets of the third and fourth books are from one another, there is nevertheless some sort of a connection between them; or, perhaps, it would be better to say there is a link between the two books.   To me, however, it looks very like the links between the different stories in Ovid's 'Metamorphoses;' links which belong to the artificial concatenation of the narrative, rather than to any natural cohesion between the parts of the subject-matter.   There is a reference to his former condition, and there is a speech in justification of his conduct; for less than this we can scarcely expect.   Then there is the forging of a shield; no ordinary piece of armour.   On it are represented all the events of his previous life, with wonderful minuteness, and in the exact order of their occurrence.   The description in Saxo is well nigh as elaborate as the work of the metallurgist.   In the details it reminds us of the two famous shields of the Iliad and the Æneid, and of more than one magic mirror.   The present writer compares it with the more truly Scandinavian Brosinga-mén.

His court in Denmark being now established with more than ordinary magnificence, in strong contrast to the squalour and misery of his days of his persecution, and, a trusty friend being chosen, Hamlet has now only to visit England and return with his wife, sure of a welcome from her royal father.   But here his

E

troubles are destined to begin afresh, and the connection between the two books is closer than it has been. It possibly may be called organic. At the same time the events that follow might have easily been narrated without it.

There was a solemn pact and promise between his father-in-law and his uncle Fengo, that if one of them died a violent death, the other should avenge it. But here it is a son-in-law who should be the victim. Nevertheless, the king makes his choice between his duty and his affections, and resolves to plot against the life of Hamlet.

Throwing off the squalor of his previous life, he is now, with the limitation of Roric's suzerainty, the Prince of Denmark. He has only to visit his wife and her royal father to be made welcome; but here comes in the pact. The king of England and Fengo were pledged to avenge the death of the first who should die, should the death be a violent one. So after a struggle of conflicting feelings, the claims of friendship, and the sanctity of promises of the kind prevailed, and it is settled that Hamlet shall be made away with, but not by Fengo's own hand. There is a terrible female in Scotland, queen and virgin, fair of face, fierce of temper, strong and dangerous, hating marriage and scorning men; and above all things, formidable, if not fatal, to such as are tempted to court her. Her will the king,—for he is a widower, woo by proxy; in which capacity Hamlet is sent forth.

So Hamlet proceeds, with something between an army and a retinue, to Scotland, where he falls asleep. There is a pleasant dale, and he puts his shield under his head, with the letters in his pocket, and falls into

a mid-day slumber. The gist of the letters are what
we anticipate—a death-warrant to the bearer. But
the virago queen sees him as he dozes, and sends a
crafty knave with orders to pluck the shield from the
back of his head, and to fetch the letters from his
side. This he does, and they are read by his mistress.
Then her real nature comes out. It is only *old* men
she dislikes, and Hamlet is not old. The letters have,
of course, been previously altered, to the effect that
she is to be wooed by the bearer. To this she has
no objection. What she now lays upon her scout is
a difficult task; he must take the letters and put
them back where he found them, also the shield,
Meanwhile Hamlet has become awake—widely so.
So when the scout returns and puts both letters and
shield in the original proper places, Hamlet is still,
to all appearances, asleep; but as soon as they are replaced, the unfortunate adventurer is made prisoner;
whereon Saxo avails himself, as usual, of the opportunity, and praises the wisdom of his hero, who at
once visits the famous virago—*regina penates accedit.*

Him the queen receives graciously, explaining the
folly of being bound in such a link as that of matri-
mony to a female who has no high blood; beauty,
perhaps, she may have, but blood is what a hero
ought to look to. She precludes denial, "Hortatur
itaque, ut placendi studium in se transferat, in se
votum nuptiale deflectat, genusque formæ præferre
discat. Hoc dicens astrictis in eum complexibus
ruit."

Still, he has to return to England; and this he
does with a retinue fully sufficient for a suite, but
not adequate to the duties of an army. They halt

within a certain distance of the wife's and father-in-law's capital. Now the wife (the real and original wife) is tender-minded, and condones, as far as may be, her husband's second marriage. She has, or is about to have, a child. But the danger to Hamlet is from her father.

Hamlet, who was sent as a proxy, had won, not only a second wife, but won her under the guise of a principal. Let the son-in-law be on his guard against the father-in-law. Hamlet is not the man to need advice on such a point as this; so, when his first wife's father asks him to a feast, he puts a coat of armour under his clothes. He is, of course, stabbed at; indeed, slightly wounded.

Hostility is thus declared; when Hamlet, who has the scout who stole and replaced the shield and the letters in his power, sends him back to the Queen (her name, as might have been stated before, is Hermentruda), who must now defend herself as best she may. But the Scotch guards are evidently too weak for the occasion. So Hamlet makes the dead help the living. There had been a preliminary skirmish, in which Hamlet lost what men went with him when he parted with his second wife to parley with the first. Of these he collects the corpses; and, partly by sticking them to stones, partly by propping them up with stakes, and partly by fixing them on horses, makes thereby a show of living men. By this the battle is won, or rather the English are made afraid of fighting one. After this Hamlet returns in triumph to Denmark, where his history becomes mixed with that of Vikletus. The question as to the real nature of Horvendil's authority in Jutland can scarcely

be dealt with seriously. This only is certain, that to
the authority of Röric Vikletus succeeds; that he
ejects his sister Grytha, Hamlet's mother, and (as we
may call her) the vice-regent of Jutland, from her
government, and that harshly, charging Hamlet with
having encroached upon the rights of the true king,
the king of Leire. And this he does with impunity,
for Hamlet (even in the fourth book an adept in
dissimulation) returns good for evil, and sends to
Vikletus rich gifts, the fruits of more than one vic-
tory. But he is only biding his time; for, as soon as
Vikletus becomes involved with enemies in other
quarters, Hamlet attacks and defeats him,—not, however, finally. By means of alliances in Scone and
Sealand, Vikletus raises an army so strong as to
make Hamlet's case desperate. And, in truth, the
hero himself well nigh despairs. He knows that if
he fight he must die, and communes much within
himself whether he should die or yield. Much, too,
as he thinks of himself, he thinks more of his wife.
But she urges him to resistance: she will join him
in the battle, and fight and die with her dear husband. Hamlet, kind, thoughtful, and practical, thinks
how, before his death, he can find a second husband
for her; and with these and other tender thoughts in
his head, he fights a battle against Viklet, in which
he is killed. His widow can now choose for herself,
and her choice is Viklet, the slayer of her husband,
—" ultro in victoris prædam amplexumque successit."
After this Viklet reigned long and quietly.

When Vikletus dies, Vermundus, his son, succeeds
him; Vermundus being stricken in years before he
himself becomes a father. At length, however, a

son is born to him, and he is named Uffo. Now
Uffo, though strong in body, was slow and dull in
spirit, so much so as to be thought unfit for either
royal or princely duties. He never laughed; rarely
spoke; took pleasure in nothing. Such was Uffo in
his youth. His father, however, marries him to the
daughter of Frovinus (Freawine), governor (*præfectus*)
of Sleswick, whose two sons are named Keto and
Vigo.

There are two great wars during the reign of
Vermund. In the first, against Athislas, king of
Sweden. Frovinus is killed; his death, however, is
revenged upon Athislas by his son Keto, supported
by Vermund. The second was against the king of
Saxony, who, when Vermund had become very old and
nearly blind, suggested that, as the father was super-
annuated, and the son, Uffo, little better than an
idiot, he (the king of Saxony) should be entrusted
with the management of the kingdom of Denmark.
If this request were denied he would lead an army
against the old king and his son, or he would challenge either to single combat. We may guess what
will happen. Uffo, under the stress of circumstances
and the stimulus of danger, will not only speak, but
speak and act to some purpose. He takes up the
king of Saxony's challenge, and kills him in a *holm-
gang*, on an island in the Eyder, near a spot where
the town of Rendsburg now stands. After Uffo's
return and triumph, and when gaxony is added to
the Danish dominions, Vermundus dies, and Uffo
succeeds him. How little he did as king, and how
he was also called Olaus Mansuetus, we have already
seen.

We have also already seen that the triple sequence of Wiglaf, Wærmund, and Offa occurs not only in Beowulf, but in the Anglo-Saxon genealogies. We shall now find the double sequence of Wærmund and Offa elsewhere. The lives of two kings, each a king of Mercia, each connected with the abbey ot St. Alban's, and each named Offa, may be found in the Appendix to Watts's edition of Mathew Paris, the heading of the two texts (so suspiciously alike are the biographies) being " Vita Regis Offæ I., cui simillima est Vita Offæ II."

Offa I. is the son of Vermund, the king of the West Angles, and the founder of Warwick, Caer Warmund, or Curia Warmundi. Rigan, who is also called Aliel, one of his nobles, aims at the succession, suggesting that Offa is little better than an idiot, as was actually the case. Rigan now threatens war, having vainly tried to get Vermund to adopt him. Offa's affliction, unlike Hamlet's, was real and physical, for he was a born blind child up to his seventh, and a born mute up to his thirteenth year. Under the stress of the danger that terrified his father, he both speaks rationally and acts effectively. Thus encouraged, Vermund collects his soldiers, crosses the Avon, conquers his enemies, and names that part of the river which runs by Rug*by* (a Danish name) *Rigan*burn, or *Rigan's* Brook. He then resigns, and dies at Gloucester.

Offa I., his son and successor, was one day hunting in a forest, and having met a lady of wonderful beauty, discovers that she is the daughter of the king of York. Her he makes his wife and queen. Soon after this, the king of Northumberland, attacked by the king of Scotland, but assisted by Offa, fights and wins a great battle. Then Offa's messenger, at or on his way to York, being either drunk or drugged, is robbed of his letters, for which (a thrice-told tale) others are substituted, to the effect that Offa's wife is to be exposed in a forest with her hands and feet cut off,—she and her children. These last are cruelly slaughtered, but the mother is spared on account of her beauty. A hermit, however, brings them back to life, and orders Offa to build a cenobium at St. Alban's. This is neglected till the time of

OFFA II.,

a saint rather than a hero. His parents present him in the church, and promise that, when able, he shall make good the neglect of his predecessor. He was a cripple rather than a mute. His wife's name was, at first, Petronilla, afterwards *Dryda*, or Quæn*drida* (*Drida* the Queen). She had been guilty of some great crime on the Continent, and was drifted to the coast of England in a boat without rigging as a punishment. She called herself a kinswoman of Charles, the king of the Franks. A wicked and deceitful woman, she contrives the murder of Albert, whom Offa meant for his son-in-law, by making a couch over a trap-door, under which was a pit. Tempted to recline on the couch, he is let down and smothered. The queen, who for her punishment is confined in a solitary retreat, is at last killed by robbers, and thrown into a pit, even as she had, herself, the sainted Albert.

The following are the texts which give us the three varieties of the physical and mental ailments of the three Offas:—

Hic Uffo coævos quosque corporis habitu supergressus, adeo hebetis ineptique animi principio juventæ existimatus est, ut privatis de publicis rebus inutilis videretur. Siquidem ab ineunte ætate numquam lusus aut joci consuetudinem præbuit, adeoque humanæ delectationis vacuus fuit, ut labrorum continentiam jugi silenti premeret, severitatem oris a ridendi prorsus officio temperaret Uffo, qui forte cum cœteris aderat, responsionis a patre licentiam flagitabat, subitoque velut ex muto vocalis evasit.

Saxo; Historia Danica, lib. iv.

OFFA I. (*Vita Regis Offæ I.*)

Licet enim idem unicus filius ejus Offa, vel Offanus, nomine, statura fuisset procerus, corpore integer, et elegantissimæ formæ juvenis existeret, permansit tamen a nativitate visu privatus usque ad annum septimum. Mutus autem et verba humana non proferens, usque ad annum ætatis suæ tricesimum.

OFFA II. (*Vita Regis II.*)

Natus est igitur memorati Tuinfrido (qui de stemmate Regum fuit) filius videlicit Pineredus, usque ad annos adolescentiæ, inutilis poplitibis contractis, et qui nec oculorum vel aurium plene officio naturali fungeretur. Unde patri suo Tuinfrido et matri suæ Marcellinæ, oneri fuit non honori, confusioni et non exultationi. Et licet filius unicus eis fuisset, mallent prole caruisse, quam talem habuisse.

The following, referring to the Uffo of Saxo, now Uffo the Strong, invests him with the character of his manhood :—

Uffo Starke a septimo ætatis anno usque ad trigesimum noluit loqui, quousque in loco, qui adhuc *Kunengicamp* dicitur, super Eydoram, cum filio regis Teutonicorum et meliore pugili totius Teutoniæ solus certans ambos occidit, et sic conditione utriusque gentis Teutonia Danis jam quarto tributaria facta est.[12]—*Chronicon Erici Regis.*

The extract which indicates his gluttony and love of the kitchen has been already given (p. 40).

OLAF KYRRE.

Olaf *Kyrre* is a cotemporary of William the Conqueror; his historian, Snorro Sturleson, of Henry II. Nevertheless, near as the two dates are to one another, the Saga is anything but historical. A portion of it has certainly a thoroughly historical look; indeed, it savours of even what is called the Philosophy of History. The king is praised as the upholder, if not the founder, of what we should now call a Peace Policy. He let well alone, taking

---

[12] Though not named, Vermund is the " Blind King " in Uhland's ballad so named, and Uffo his son. The name of the sword was *Skrep.*

(3.)

> Noch stehn die Fechter alle stumm;
> Tritt keiner aus sein Reihn.
> Der blinde König kehrt sich um;
> " Bin ich denn ganz allein ?
> Da sasst des Vaters Rechte
> Sein junger Sohn so warm :
> " Vergönn' mir's, das ich fechte !
> Wohl fühle ich Kraft im Arm."

(4.)

> " O Sohn, der Feind is Riesenstark,
> Ihm hielt noch Keiner Stand ;
> Und, doch, in dir ist edles Mark,
> Ich fühl's am Druck der Hand.
> Nimm, hier, *die alte** Klinge ;*
> Sie ist der Skalden Preiss ;
> Und, fällst Du, so verschlinge
> Die Fluth mich armen Greiss."

* The name of this sword was *Screp.*

matters easily. He "was called by some Olaf Kyrre,
but by many Olaf the Bonder" (yeoman), "because
he sat in peace, without strife, within or without the
country, and gave no reasonable cause for others to
plunder his dominions."[13] Several of the Norwegian
towns made, in his reign, a start in what we now call
Municipal Institutions. It is scarcely a refinement
to suggest that this looks like the opinion of men
who looked back upon a time when a system of law
and commerce began to develope itself at the expense
of an age of insecure heroism, without considering
very nicely how much was due to age and how much
to the ruler. If there is something indefinite about
this, there is nothing either vague or hazy in the
delineation of his character as an individual. He
was a thorough Norseman, with a fair skin and flaxen
hair. He was very silent, except when in his cups,
and then he was talkative : and he was talkative
very often.

Such, then, is the general view of him as a
politician ; such the personal description of him,
mind and body, as an individual. In his Saga, however, all this is dispatched in little more than a page.
The remainder has a very tralaticious look. He
builds a church at Nidaros (Drontheim), and places
the altar over the very spot where his predecessor,
St. Olave, was buried. Here miracles take place,
and a blind man sees, and a dumb man sings.

Then he has a conversation with a peasant, who
professes to understand the language of birds. The
king doubts, but the peasant convinces him.

Then he is a reformer in the domestic economy of

[13] Laing, translator of the Heimskringla, Saga ix.

drinking. Before his time the fire seems to have been in the middle of the room, with a bench on each side of it. The king sat in the middle of one of them, and when he had taken his turn at the drinking-horn, had to pass it across the fire to the guest opposite. Olaf arranged the benches so that they ran round, rather than across, the fire.

Surely we have read of something like all this before,—of that mixture of wisdom and folly which the habit of never speaking except when at the wine-cup so naturally suggests; of that unregal acquaintance with the affairs of the kitchen; and, above all, of the speaking of the dumb man.

Indeed, this carries us farther to a comparison between Olaf as a restorator of the shrine at Drontheim, and Offa in the same, or a similar, at St. Albans. The understanding of the language of birds is too common an element in fiction to claim much attention. It occurs, however, with something more than ordinary prominence in both " Oswald " and " Erendil " romances of the Hamlet Cycle.

This, however, only brings him within the wide and indefinite domain of fiction. What can we find that brings in special contact with England ? What insight do we get as to the introduction of the word Cwiran, or Cuaran into the British Islands ? Olaf Kyrre never set foot upon any of them. It is possible, however, that there was never a time when the name, or even the nickname, of a king in Norway was more likely to be formidable in England than it was in the time of Olaf Kyrre. In his Saga there are three quotations, after Snorro's practice, of Scaldic poems. They are the last we have. The

names of the particular Skalds are given :—Stuf and
Stein; the son of Hurdiss—Hurdisarson. They must
have been cotemporaries. In two of them is de-
cribed as the king who, without fighting, *frightened*
England. And of the terror thus suggested, we
have, within England itself, ample evidence. Olaf
was the son of the Harald Hardrada who was defeated by Harald Godvinsson, as he is called, at
Stamford Bridge, just before the Battle of Hastings.
To ensure against the attempts on the part of his
son, Olaf Kyrre, one-third of Yorkshire was laid
waste. This is the English account. On the side of
Scandinavia, we have, in Olaf's Saga, a dialogue
between him and Canute of Denmark. Canute pro-
poses an invasion of England, giving Olaf the choice
of supplying sixty ships, and letting him (Canute)
command, or *vice versâ*. In the Dialogue Olaf gives
his reasons for declining the command and for supplying the ships instead. He remarks, truly enough,
that the Canute family have been lucky in England,
the Olaf family the contrary. Surely, then, there
was something to make the name of Olaf Kyrre
familiar in the parts north of the Humber.

The devastation of Yorkshire is a measure of this
for England; the whole tone of Olaf Kyrre's Saga
for Scandinavia. Even the dates have an English
foundation. When the cotemporary kings of Denmark are mentioned, the first of them is mentioned
as having died ten years after the death of the two
Haralds, *i. e.* Harald Hardrade of Norway, and Harold,
the son of Godwin of England, but the names in full
are not given; they are simply the Two Haralds.
The reader supplied the rest. There is also a curious

piece of Greek learning. The drinking that Olaf, the Kitchen King, altered is called a *Trapeza* (τρά-πεζα). This is meant to anticipate an objection. Snorro is writing (there or thereabouts) a hundred years, and no more, after the real rule of a real king of Norway; yet this is how he writes. If the confusion, here assumed, between a Hamlet who was originally Chochilaicus and Hamlet who was originally Olaus, actually took place, it is too near the historical period to be probable. The word *Kyrre* is to find its way from Olaf, of Norway, to Olaf, or Anlaf, of England or Ireland; to be extended from him to Havelok, and to give us all the results here submitted to the reader. The time is too short, or if not too short too late, *i. e.* too near the time of genuine history for such confusion to take root. It looks like this at the first view, especially if we mean that Havelok had never been named Cuaran until Anlaf had been so named before him, and that Anlaf had never been so called until after the time of Olaf Kyrre; in fact, that the Anlaf Cwiran of the year A.D. 950, of the Anglo-Saxon Chronicle, was not so called until after the end of the tenth century. Yet this is what the present writer means. The date, however, of an event is one thing, the date of an entry (as already stated) another.

It is only in two out of seven manuscripts of the Anglo-Saxon Chronicle that this adjunct is found; the two which have been already quoted. In the others, though the event is entered there is no such name as Cwiran; and that the two which contain it are subsequent to the death of Olaf Kyrre is collected from the opinion of Mr. Thorpe. Both copies are in the hand of the *twelfth* century; and, except that in the Bodleian MS., the hand and ink vary a little, A.D. 1122, the writing is uniform.

There is no evidence, then, of the name *Curran* or *Cuaran* being necessarily earlier than the time of Olaf Kyrre. It may, however, have been so, inasmuch as there may have been two persons who bore it. It is also possible that the words may be different.

Now this is a question which, for the full exhibition of the present doctrine, it is necessary to investigate, and it is not pretended that it can be settled conclusively. It is moreover admitted, or rather proclaimed, that the general opinion is at least against Anlaf *Cwiran* having taken his second name from Olaf *Kyrre*. How far the two words are the same, or different, is another question. It is only, however, for the establishment of certain corollaries from the present train of argument that the identification is required. The main fabric can stand either with or without it. The confusion between Havelok Curran and Anlaf Cwiran is simply a matter of fact which stands upon its own merits. By the deduction of the name from Olaf Kyrre we can explain it. Without him it is unexplained; it may or may not be inexplicable. However, whether explained, unexplained, or inexplicable, it is equally a matter of fact.

The bearing of this is upon the fixation of one of the two names of Saxo's Uffo; for we have seen that Uffo is said by Saxo to have been also called Olaus *Mansuetus*. Uffo then is in Norse *Olaf*, just like Olaf *Kyrre*, and *Anlaf (i. e. Olaf) Cwiran*. What is he in Norse as *Mansuetus?* That depends on the translators of the word. It is the same of *Kyrre?*—

That depends on the translator also; for there is more
than one word by which the Latin *Mansuetus* can be
rendered into Norse, and more than one word by
which the Norse *Kyrre* can be rendered into Latin;
while it so happens that it is a Latin writer, Saxo, from
whom we first get *Mansuetus,* and a Norse one, Saxo,
from whom we first get *Kyrre.* How each of these
writers would have translated his own term no one
knows. We only know that Saxo derives the epithet
from the mildness of his hero's natural temper, and
Snorro from his peaceful policy. It is needless, after
this, to say that *Kyrre* and *Mansuetus*, if not the
natural, patent, and unequivocal translations of one
another, are allied in their signification. They are
represented, however, by different words; the Danish
for Olaus *Mansuetus* is Olaf *Litillate,* the Latin
for Olaf *Kyrre* is Olaus *Tranquillus.* It cannot be
denied that, as far as the difference goes, it implies a
difference between the two Olafs. As for Anlaf
Cwiran, he is nowhere, since it is only in the Anglo-
Saxon Chronicle, in the Irish Annals, and in the
French Romance that his second name appears; in
other words, *Cwiran* or *Cuaran* is no Norse term at
all, and this has been one of the reasons for bringing
in Olaf Kyrre. It is with him, and him only, that
Uffo as a Scandinavian is to be compared. Offa,
indeed, may be compared with Anlaf Cwiran, and
though this increases the confusion it strengthens the
argument; for the primary assumption is that from first
to last there is confusion, and nothing but confusion.

The difference, then, between Olaus *Mansuetus*
Olaus *Tranquillus,* or Olaf *Litillate* and Olaf *Kyrre* is
unimportant. The real, undoubted, and historical

Olaf is one—Olaf *Kyrre*. Yet the distinction could scarcely fail to develop itself. In the first place, the translation was a *cross* one, *Mansuetus* had to be translated into Norse, *Kyrre* into Latin, and that by different and independent translators. Nothing, then, is more natural than the two approximate synonyms, Tranquillus and Mansuetus: and the doctrine that they applied to two different individuals is equally so; at least, it would be so in the eyes of Scandinavian logographers in the twelfth century. They worked apart from each other, and had few authorities to help them. Saxo, for instance, in the very case before us, is writing a history of the most Southern, Snorro one of the most Northern, Kingdoms of Scandinavia, Their materials, however, are to a great extent common to Denmark, Norway, and Sweden. Meanwhile, it is from Denmark that Saxo and from Iceland that Snorro is writing. It is not, then, too much to say that, when, under such circumstances two different names occur, the inference that there were two different bearers of them presents itself as a matter of course. When our data are sufficient, or, in other words, we are engaged on a true historical period, this error can, of course, be corrected ; or, rather, it corrects itself. If it were not so we should have as many Charleses of Burgundy and Louises of France and Germany as there are real or apparent synonyms for the words Temeraire and Debonnair. Olaus Mansuetus, then, as a King of Denmark, exists only so far as he is an *alias* of Uffo, and Uffo, in the united character of Dane and King, is merely Olaus Mansuetus under an *alias*. There are real Uffos, and there is one real Olaf the Mild, Tranquil, Peaceful or the like : but

F

they are not the Uffo or Olaus Mansuetus of Saxo.
It is, however, on the definite authority of Saxo that
the two are identified. To this the attention of the
reader is again directed. The connexion between
Olaf the Mansuete, Olaf the Tranquil, Olaf Kyrre,
and Anlaf Cwiran is inferential; and it is the present writer who suggests it. The identification of
Olaus Mansuetus and Uffo is a matter of evidence
—good or bad as the case may be—but still evidence
as opposed to inference, and authority as opposed to
speculation, On what *data* the statement of Saxo
rests I am not prepared to say. I only insist upon
the fact of its being Saxo's; and, as such, I take it as
I find it. It leads me, as we have seen, to the Anlaf
Cwiran of the Anglo-saxon Chronicle, and the Amblaibh Cuaran of Ireland; and here for the present
I leave it; with a repetition of the remark that contact with Anlaf Cwiran is much the same as contact with Havelok the Dane.

The Amlethus of Saxo, we must remember, is, by
the present doctrine, not one individual but two, one
of whom is the Amlethus of the Third, the other
the Amlethus of the Fourth, Book. Now great
prominence has been given to the fact that, while
the Amlethus of the Third Book is a pretending
madman, there is, to say the least, mental malady of
some sort in no less than three Offas. The character
of this differs with the individual; but, in all, it is
only temporary; Amlethus, Uffo, and both the Offas,
like snakes that cast their skins, all come out, at
their proper time, as strong and wise men. Now,
just as the *alias* Olaus Mansuetus brings the Uffo of
Saxo into contact with Havelok, so does this com-

mon trait of mental derangement, more or less unreal, bring the same Uffo (the Uffo who is Olaus) into contact with the Hamlet of the Third Book, or the Hamlet of Shakespear.

The approximation, then, of Uffo—Olaus Mansuetus, to Amlethus, as name and name, coincides with the approximation of Uffo to Amlethus, as man and man; and in this coincidence lies the great importance of every relation to Uffo. So far as he is Olaus Mansuetus he has brought us into contact with Anlaf Cwiran, and, so far as he is the Amlethus of the Third Book, he has carried the Hamlet of Shakespear along with him.

The Amlethus of Saxo (we must reiterate our formula) is not one individual, but two; one of whom, the Amlethus of the Third Book and of Shakespear, we have compared with Offa, who is Olaus Mansuetus. In the Amlethus of the Fourth Book; it is submitted that we have Hugletus (*melius* Huglekus), Higelac, and Chochilaicus. The history of Chochilaicus, so long as it keeps free from that of Offa, etc., is comparatively simple. The agreement, name for name, and man for man, between Chochilacius and Higelac, has long been recognized; and it is to the historical Chochilaicus that the legend of the bones of Hiuglauc has always been referred. The Swedish Huhleikr of Snorro, and the Irish Huglekus of Saxo have never been separated from either one another or from Chochilaicus; though the distortion of their respective histories is considerable. Of Hugletus the son of the Dan II., the hero, so to say, of the present treatise, little has hitherto been said either way; for without some such doc-

trine as the one here advanced there is next to
nothing to say about him. His name is here
changed to Huglekus on purely palæographic
grounds; or by a simple piece of commonplace
emendatory criticism. It is, then, by hypothesis,
put in the place of that of the Amlethus of the
Fourth Book, thus implying a confusion between
two individuals, rather than a mere change in the
form of a word. On the other hand, word for word,
Havelok is held to be Higelac; and this brings us
exactly to the point where the line which begins
with Chochilaicus meets the line which begins with
Olaus Mansuetus (Uffo) ; where, as we have
already stated, the same individual is in two places
mentioned as Hanelok; in the one of which the word
stands for Havelok the Dane, and in the other for
Anlaf Cwiran. Out of this come, (as *words*,) those
forms like Amblaibh, Amelaus, Amelaivus, and
the like, which made such a form as Amlethus possible. It does not come from Olaf and it does not
come from Higelac purely and simply; nor does it
come from any letter-change between word and
word. By a confusion between them, as man and
man, the bearers of names as different as Olaf and
Higelac, take a form out of which Amlethus is a
probable educt.

This confusion between Havelok and Anlaf, etc.,
like that of Olaf, rests, not upon inference, but evidence; and it is upon this undoubted confusion, or
rather upon the complex character of it, that the
leading elements of the present criticism mainly
rest. We have seen how far, as the pretending mad-

man, the Amlethus of the Third Book agrees with
Offa. We have, also, seen how decided are the
relations of the Amlethus of the Fourth Book with
Viklet, Vermund, and Offa. They are nearly, those
of Higelac *minus* the difference of the name. But
Amlethus is no name at all for any single individual;
the name which it is substituted for being *Huglekus.*
Upon this substitution the whole question turns; for
it will scarcely be denied that when, form for form,
Hugletus is changed to Huglekus, and, name for
name, Huglekus for Amlethus, the sequence (1)
Huglekus, (2) Vikletus, (2) Vermundus, and (4)
Uffo, in Saxo, and the association, in Beowulf, of (1)
Higelac, (2) Wiglaf, (3) Wærmund, and (4) Offa tell
their own story. What, then, becomes of Amlethus?
The answer to this is that he is just explained away
altogether; improved off the face of the earth; or
(to go further into the over-familiar language of
the day) made to " disappear into space."

Nor is this strange. On the contrary, his absolute
abolition is the one thing needful. As has been so
often said, *Amlethus* is no man's name; but the name
of a pair of men. *This* dictum is the present
writer's; but the dictum that neither, man for man,
nor, name for name, is a second Amlethus to be
found in the whole range of Scandinavian myth,
legend, or literature, is *not* the present writer's. It
is the express statement of Saxo's editor Müller; and
that not as a mere incidental remark, but as the
result of careful search for instances to the contrary.
Something, indeed, of the kind he found; but he especially commits himself to the positive assertion that

whatever in Scandinavian is Amlethian is merely a reproduction of the Saxonian Amlethus.

It is now submitted that, when, slightly. changing the subject and taking Saxo's list from another point of view, we may, from the series that gives us *Amlethus*, also get *Humblus*, i.e., as a word which the Anglo-Irish metamorphoses of the name *Olaf* may legitimately be supposed to supply; and with this we may consider the relations of Dan as the eponymus of Denmark, and Chochilaicus as the first historical Dane. In Saxo's list Götricus is the thirty-eighth name; and, at the same time, the only one against which no objections as to its genuine historical character can be raised. *Nearly* in the middle of the list come (17) Uffo, (18) Dan II, (19) Hugletus (*mel.* Huglekus); and, then, at the very beginning of it (1) Humble I, (2) Dan, (3) Humble II. Now, Dan is the eponymus of Denmark; and, as such, in all the dynasties has his name at, or near, the top of the list. It is not necessarily *quite* at the top; and this is because, unless he be an autochthon, he must have a parent; a parent who in certain cases, must be put forward conspicuously. When two nations, for instance, profess to derive their origin from two brothers, the name of the common ancestor forces itself upon the logographer, The Danes and English came from Dan and Angle, who were brothers. But who was the father of Dan and Angle? Whoever he was he was a *pro*-eponymus; and, as Dan, *whenever it may occur*, is an eponymic, the name of his father is a *pro*-eponymic, term.

The facts that determine the names of *pro*-eponymi are numerous; and there is no place in the present treatise for discussing them at large. It is only certain that one of them is the date of the first authentic name in the history of the country under notice. When this is not only sufficiently early, but, likewise, so isolated as to stand without any others in immediate contact, there is every chance of his being made either the father or the son of the eponymus; and, when there are more lists than one, he may appear the father in the first, and the son, in the second; or *vice versá*; and, more than this, when this conflict, comes under the scrutiny of a fresh logographer he may appear, in the way of a compromise, in both characters; just as we have it here—Humblus I, Dan, Humblus II.

Again, the name of the eponymus may be repeated; and it is submitted that when it shows itself at anything like equal intervals, and in lists containing a mixture of new and old names, the chances are that two lists have been fused into one. If the proeponymus re-appears as well, the chances are improved; and still more closely do they approach to certainty when the pro-eponymus is both father and son. Now this, according to the *aliases* that we have just investigated, is the case with

1 Humble I.
2 Dan I.   and 17 Uffo
3 Humble II.   18 Dan II.
                     19 Hugletus (i.e., Huglekus).

Huglekus, though it has the additional complication of the ambiguity of the word Humblus, which may be an *alias* of either Anlaf Cwiran, or Havelok, or the one in one of its places, and the other in the other, is repeated. Still whatever may be the explanation of the details of the repetition of this triad, the

repetition of the confusion of the names is undoubted.

In Chochilaicus we get a date (A.D. 516), a place,
and historical evidence that before, as well as after,
the time of Charlemagne there were Danish piracies
in districts as near to England as the Netherlands;
or, in other words, on the opposite side of the German Ocean. How far this raises a presumption in
favour of similar ones in Britain is a point upon
which there may be a difference of opinion. If the
history of our island, for the sixth century, were so
full and authentic as to make the fact of nothing
whatever being said about them evidence of their
actual non-existence, the presumption would be a
very slight one indeed. No such history, however,
exists. Our best authority for anything like detail
in this very obscure period is Beda, whose history is
not less than two centuries later; and the utmost we
get from this against such a presumption is his notice
of the languages spoken in our island, in which Danish
is not mentioned. But it is only a Danish settlement
of a certain magnitude and permanence that this ex-
cludes. In the first half of the tenth century, we
get the name Higelac, and associated with it that
of Hengest as an early contemporary. Hence, while
the name points to Chocilaicus, the date and connexion suggest England; while, in respect to his
own connexions, Higelac is, perhaps, more of a Dane
than an Englishman. As far as he is concerned,
there is nothing that militates against his historical
character; for though Grendel, the water-fiend, and
the fire-drake, belong to the story of Beowulf, Higelac
is mentioned in the poem only as the friend, kinsman,
and lord of that hero.

The middle of the century brings us to the reign of Athelstan, under whom the Danes of the Carlovingian (as opposed to the Merovingian) period are as famous as they are formidable. We have numerous names, but any name like Havelok is conspicuous for its absence. It is plain, however, that if the origin of the legend of *Havelok*, the Danes, and the Lincolnshire belief about the foundation of the town of Grimsby, are to be investigated at all, the date, name, and country of any one name anything like *Higelac* must enter into the inquiry. Unless we can find a Havelok in either the tenth century or the centuries that follow, we must either ignore the question of his historical reality, or look to some earlier period. The name, however, of Havelok has not yet occurred, nor will it for the next two centuries. Nevertheless, the middle of the tenth century is the most important point in the history of the name. Then it was that the Anlaf who is supposed to have taken to himself the personality of Higelac, so far as he was Chochilaicus, on the one side, and of Uffo, so far as he was Olaus Mansuetus, on the other, and out of whose name, in its Irish form, *Amlethus*, as a word, is maintained to be an educt, lived and died; claiming for himself the title of king both in Northumberland and Ireland. Here, however, there are, at least, three complications. In the first place there are more bearers of the name than one; in the second, the real and exact sound and spelling of the name are uncertain; and, thirdly, the date of his life and death is nearly two hundred years earlier than the names for the extraordinary transformations of which it accounts, inasmuch as the historical notices which first give us the important forms, Havelok, Amblaibh, Amlethus, Cuaran, and Cwiran, are all later than the beginning of the twelfth century.

1. There are *two* Anlafs in the time of Athelstan. One is killed in the Battle of Brunanburg, and this is not the one who becomes Anlaf Cwiran. The one who becomes Anlaf Cwiran was the son of Sidroc, or Sydaracus. Of the ordinary English histories the fullest account of him is in Lappenberg; of original sources, the fullest is the Irish History, published under the Master of the Rolls, and edited by Mr. Stewart, entitled 'The Wars of the Gael and Saxon.' Here his name is spelt *Amlaf*.

2. *Anlaf* and Anelaf are the forms of the name in the 'Anglo-Saxon Chronicle'; and the current opinion as to the nature of sounds of A and N by which it is distinguished from *Olaf* is that the one form is Anglo-Saxon, the other Danish. Practically, this is the case. There is no evidence, however, that, at the time of the Anlafs, the name Olaf had a concurrent existence; since, the Scandinavian notices are one and all more than a century and a half later than that of the fuller and stronger form in N. Hence, it is probable that the two forms differed from another as older and newer, rather than as English and Norse. If so, the Anlafs, Norsemen as they were, may have called themselves what they were called by the English.

3. The difference between the date of Anlaf as a king in the British Isles, and the date of the confusion of names is necessary to be attended to, lest we attribute the transformation to a condition rather

than to its direct and efficient cause. The direct and efficient cause was the uncritical and imperfect knowledge of the writers of the twelfth century; and the existence of the Anlafs of Ireland and Northumberland was merely the condition which made such errors possible. The same applies to Olaf *Kyrre.* It was through him that the form *Cuaran* took birth. It was the inaccuracy of the age that transferred it to some one else; and, then, not satisfied with doing this, made two different kings out of the two quasi-synonymous translations of it. Olaf Kyrre is the contemporary of William the Conqueror; Anlaf, of Athelstan and his two successors. During the interval, no such name as Amblaibh, Olaf, or Havelok occurs. They all belong to the twelfth century, and all crop out within a few years of both one another and other names indicative of similar confusion. They are all connected with the same system. Nevertheless, the deduction of Cuaran from Olaf Kyrre is not absolutely necessary to the argument; it only *accounts* for the confusion. But, whether accounted for or not, the confusion still exists.

A similar remark applies to another metamorphosis; viz.—that of the " Haneloke that wedded Goldesburge," and the Hanelocke[14] who was cotemporary with Conelocke. Here Havelok the Dane is held to pass into Anlaf Cwiran. By assuming, however, a little more confusion, the process may be reversed; in which it is *out of* Anlaf Cwiran that Havelok the Dane is evolved. In either case, however, the con-

---

[14] See pp. 33, 34. See also, for the extent to which Havelok the Dane has, actually, been identified with Anlaf Cwiran, Sir Frederick Madden's Introduction to his edition of the Romances of that name.

fusion remains; and for the purpose of the present
work, which is mainly an investigation of the rules
by which Saxo Grammaticus should be read, it
matters little which view we take. In a question as
to Lincolnshire legends, and the relation of Havelok
to the town of Grimsby, the difference is, undoubtedly, important. But this is not the question now
under notice.

Within . . . . years after the death of Olaf
Kyrre comes his biography, and here, for the first
time, the word *Olaf* in the place of *Anlaf*, and the
word *Kyrre* for the first time presents itself; but the
full fountain of error and confusion is opened with
its great gush of complex blunders; blunders which
give us (1) Snorro's Huhleikr, with a history incompatible with either history or uniform fiction; (2)
Saxo's Irish Hugletus, also in disguise; (3) the at-
tachment of the legend of Rolf the Walker to the
bones of Hiuglauc; and, above all (4) Havelok the
Dane, whether as Havelok pure and simple, or as
Havelok Cuaran, with a history which, whatever it
may be, is neither that of Higelac or Chochilaicus,
nor yet that of Anlaf.

Nor is this all. I have hitherto spoken of the
two Amlethi of the two different Books of Saxo, as
wholly distinct; and, practically, or in rough way,
they are so. At any rate it is only the first of the
two that is Shakespear's 'Hamlet;' and it is only
he who agrees with the *three* Offas in a temporary
show of insanity. This, perhaps, is a sufficient characteristic. But, then, it is only to Uffo and the two
Offas, as Crown Princes or young men, that the insanity or imbecility applies. All three, when grown

up, are strong, and wise, and heroic. Hence, then, the Offas are divided into two; and it is only with one of them that Shakespear's 'Hamlet' coincides. But in the Amlethus of the Fourth Book (the Amlethus that is Higelac, etc.), there is an *Offa* element; for Higelac has apparently conjugal relations with a lady whom Thorpe treats as his wife, while Kemble says she belongs to Offa. But then this is not Offa the Crown Prince, not the Offa whom we make out to be Shakespear's 'Hamlet'; so that, though there is an Offa element in both the Amlethi, it is not an intermixture of the *same* Offa. The formula, then, is this. There are two Offas and two Hamlets; and one Offa coincides to a preponderating extent with the Amlethus, and the other with the other. The Hamlet of the Third Book has no wife; one of the Offas has a good wife, the other has a bad one. Havelok the Dane, also, has a good wife. Meanwhile, the Hamlet of the Fourth Book has two wives, one good, and one bad; and the name of the bad one is Hermen*truda*, while the bad one of the second Offa is named *Drida*, or Cwæn-*drida*. And here I leave the maze; chiefly because I think that enough has been said for the purpose of the argument; partly from the trifling character of the manipulation of the changes that this mixture of method and confusion bring about; and, partly, from sheer fatigue.

All this confusion, however, we get within eighty years of Olaf Kyrre's death; though it is the name "*Olaf Kyrre*" which has been put prominently forward as its main condition. It is a manifest objection that the interval is too short for its development. Be it so.

There is, however, an error of the same kind as one
of the details of one of the very compositions under
notice where the progress of error is quicker still. The
name of the Danish King of whom the pure and simple
Havelok of the English, (with the *Havelok Cuaran* of
French Romance), is the son, is *Birkabeyn*. The Danish
king, of whom Havelok Cuaran is the son, is *Birkbeyn*. Now, even if Havelok (Cuaran) be confounded
with Anlaf (Quiran), this name of Birkbeyn is a very
late one. The date for Anlaf, of the Anglo-Saxon
Saxon Chronicle, is A.D. 9 . . , so that he could
scarcely be the son of a father whose name appears,
for the first time, A.D. 1173, for such is the case with
Birkbeyn. And, even then, it is not the proper name
of an individual. It was the nickname for a poli-
tical faction, half military, and half predatory, that
supporting the pretensions to a man called Eystein,
who gave himself out as the son King Eystein
Haraldsson, having been defeated in the open field,
took refuge in the forests, and when their clothes
were worn out wound the bark of the birch-tree
round their legs, and were thus called *Birkebeins*, or
Birkbeiners, Birch-bones, or Birch-legs. Their oppo-
nents were the Baglers; and the time of the Baglers
and the Birkbeyns was the time of Snorro Sturleson;
so that it is under the full light of history that this
name first presents itself. Of course there may have
been Birkebeiners before; but, unless we assume
their existence, the date of the French Havelok is
the last quarter of the twelfth century at the
earliest.

Hitherto the criticism has been so variable in its
direction that it is difficult to say to what part of the

general subject it has most especially applied. Probably the largest amount of it bears upon the character of the early logography of Denmark. The poem, however, of Beowulf, along with the English and French versions of the Romance of Havelok, the Dane, has also an ample share of it. So has that part of the Heimskringla which bears upon the history of Olaf Kyrre. It is likely, however, that, notwithstanding all this, the Hamlet of Shakespear is the only point which many of my readers have cared about; and I may add, that before the subject is done with it will be the Hamlet of Shakespear which, first and last, shall have commanded the most attention on the part of the writer. To this the future discussions, which will henceforth run in a narrower and more direct channel, are now about to be exclusively directed. It cannot be said that much of what has hitherto been written comes clearly and definitely under the head of Shakespearian criticism: however much the names of Shakespear and Hamlet may be associated, and, however much it may be the case that it is mainly as a creation of Shakespear that Hamlet interests the nation at large. That the simple question of his existence or his non-existence as a personal and historical individual is one which has an interest of some kind or other, is what most of us are ready to admit. The discussion of it, however, with most of us passes for one of the curiosities in the byeways of literature rather than one for which there is any special call. It will be seen, however, in the sequel, that such a view as this does scant justice to the value of these investigations; for it is not in their bearings upon the text of Shakespear that their merits or demerits exclusively or even especially consist. "What," let us now ask, " can we claim in the way of personality of Hamlet; and what comes of such personality as we can get?" Very little indeed. In the first place the personality is no true personality at all: inasmuch as there are two Hamlets, and Shakespear's is *not* the real one. Shakespear's Hamlet, as far as he is any one at all, is Offa; but the personality of Offa himself, so far as he is Hamlet, is of a very equivocal character. His is made up of the odds and ends of tralaticious absurdities, of general, rather than particular appropriation; so that the bearer of it is a lay-figure rather than a real man in the flesh. Out of this and the like come *bi*-personalities, and *semi*-personalities which, after all, end in mere *quasi-personalities;* and a *quasi*-personality is all that be claimed for Shakespear's Hamlet, or the Amlethus of the Third Book. The Amlethus of the Fourth Book, the Hamlet who is Chochilaicus, can do more. He may pronounce himself the representative of a genuine hero. It is possible, however, that, by the mere force of genius, the equivocal Hamlet who is identified with Shakespear has in the hearts and the imaginations of men the most reality. Guarding, however, against sentiment and tall talk, let us ask what comes of the Shakespearian Hamlet as the writer leaves and as the reader finds him?

Thus much does the present dissertation suggest to us. 1. The hopelessness of expecting to find within the four corners of the English translation of Bellay's French translation of Saxo's Latin narrative, either the whole or the half of the antecedents of the

Shakespearian drama; and (2) a caution against over-refining upon the nature of Hamlet's madness. The more we isolate the narrative of Saxo, and limit our notions of his hero by the single account of him in the Historia Danica, the more freedom and latitude we allow both ourselves and the dramatist in the estimate of his character. The more, however, we recognize additional sources for his history, and the more we find that the evidence of these is uniform as to the nature of his mental ailment, the more we are constrained to treat him as a Dramatis Persona whose character has come to us, to a certain extent, ready-made; and, as such, one which is not to be either tampered with or refined upon gratuitously. Common sense tells us this, and the old Horatian rule reminds us of it. We are not to make Medea mild; nor Ino cheerful; nor Ixion an honest man; nor Io domestic; nor Orestes jovial: neither must Achilles be gentle and forgiving; but, on the contrary, passionate, vindictive, and inexorable — the moral of which is that we must think twice before, in the way of either will or intellect, we invest the weakness of Hamlet with actual or even approximate reality. The pretendedness of Hamlet's malady is as genuine as the reality of that of Orestes; and, for reasons upon which I will enlarge hereafter, I am inclined to think that long before it came under the cognizance of Shakespear his *dramatic* character was as strongly stamped and stereotyped as that of any one of the heroes or heroines in the Horatian list. This is how it came to Shakespear. Whether he took it as it came, or refined upon it, is another question; and upon this anything which relates to the form

G

taken by the story of the præ-Shakesperian Hamlet has a patent and definite bearing.

With this view I shall lay before the reader the result of my investigations upon what we may conveniently call the " *German* Hamlet ; " though, as we shall soon see, the actual title of the play is somewhat different.

A connection, of more than ordinary closeness, between the German and English theatres, towards the end of the sixteenth and at the beginning of the seventeenth centuries, has long been recognized. The interest, however, which was created by the earlier notices of it, slackened ; until, in the first quarter of the present century it was revived. With Gotsched, the most influential of the earlier critics, and his cotemporaries, it was rather a question of Shakespear's influence in Germany, than that of Germany upon England. Tieck, in 1817, reversed this view, and showed how one play, at least, illustrated Shakespear. This was the " Fair Sidea," or, " Die schöne Sidea," a play which had a common element with the Tempest.

In like manner " Much Ado About Nothing " and The " Two Gentlemen of Verona " are partially illustrated by the " *Schöne Phenicia* " and " *Julio and Hippolito* " respectively.

This gives us three plays; to which we may add, as a fourth, " *Romios and Jiuletta* "—" Romeo and Juliet," of which the exact relations to England, on one side, and to Germany, on the other, require examination.

The fifth and sixth, by which Cohn's collection is completed, are the " Fratricide's Tragedy," or, " *Der bestrafte Brudermord*," and " Titus Andronicus," and the play under notice. These derive their comparatively high importance from the extent to which, while they agree in their general character with one another, they combine, as compared with the English drama, difference with likeness, and likeness with difference, in a manner so remarkable as to make their exact relations obscure. They are neither wholly independent dramas, like the first three, nor mere reproductions, like "*Romios and Jiuletta*." Indeed what they actually are in respect to their origin remains, at least in the opinion of the present writer, to be considered.

The whole six plays are now very accessible, for they may be found not only in the German, but in an English translation, in Cohn's "Shakespear in Germany," of which the preface, or introduction, is as well worthy of a careful study as the texts which it illustrates; the information it supplies being referable to both the writers and the actors of the German stage.

Of the former, Jacob Ayrer is, upon the whole, the most important. He followed upon the model of Hans Sachs, and like him, addressed the populace at large. In common with the dramatists of the century, he was, as compared with his general influence, a man of whom we know, personally, but little. He died A.D. 1605; in 1593 he received the freedom of the city of Nuremberg, where he became proctor and notary to the Town Court. Between these two dates lie those of all his numerous compositions, so far as they are known to us. The general collection of his works, like that of Shakespear's, is posthumous; the *Opus Theatricum* being published in

1618. This contains thirty tragedies and thirty-six Shrovetide plays, with a promise of forty more. Towards this number of a hundred and six in full, only three additions have since been made. The search, however, has led to the opinion that out of the sixty-six plays of the *Opus Theatricum* no less than twenty-two were composed between '95 and '98. Two *Song-plays* (*Singenspiele*—operas) were composed in two days—a day for each.

How far the German Theatre advanced under Ayrer is not very plain. It is only safe to say that he was not an innovator; that he agreed with his predecessors more than his successors; that he carried forward and promulgated what Hans Sachs has bequeathed to him; though, as we expect beforehand, with a difference of degree.

Henry Julius, Duke of Brunswick, was *both* patron and dramatist. His life was nearly parallel with that of Shakespear. He was born a year before the English poet—*i.e.*, in 1563; and, in 1613, he died two years before him. Ten pieces have come down to us; not exactly bearing his name, but the enigmatic anagram of HIBELDEHA, meaning *H*enricus *J*ulius *B*runsvicensis, *E*t *L*uneburgensis *D*ux, *E*piscopatus *H*alberstadensis *A*ntistes. The dates of the *publication* of all these dramas lie within the years 1593 and 1594. At what previous date they were *composed* has yet to be ascertained.

As a patron, the Duke of Brunswick by no means stood alone. Maurice, the Landgrave of Hesse, was a patron also; and, though not a critic, a musician.

The main part, however, of Cohn's introduction relates to the actors rather than the composers, and

of these the history is, to a great extent, English.
Whatever may be the difficulties in accounting for it
(and more than one conjecture has been hazarded on
the question), the fact that there was at this time
more than one company of English actors in Germany, and that these carried with them the representation of English plays, is undoubted. How they
managed with the language we cannot well see.
How far they undertook German plays by writers
exclusively German, or how far they limited themselves to the compositions with which they had
become familiar in England, we do not know. We
only know that they were numerous and influential,
and that they carried with them English plays—more,
probably, in manuscript, than as printed and published
texts. We know, moreover, that some of them, at
least, returned from Germany to England early enough
to make a name on the London boards, at the time
when the best plays of Shakespear were exhibited;
and two of these we know by name. Let us also
remember that though contemporaries of Shakespear,
they are what we may call his *older* contemporaries.
They need not have been younger men. They need
only have engaged in their profession earlier.

The bearing of this diffusion of *actors* over a
country like Germany, of the return to England on
the part of many of them, and of the action and reaction thus established between the theatres of the
two countries, is by no means one of an ordinary
character. When *plays* are imported or translated
the influence of the country from which they are
introduced is plain and patent. There is, in most
cases, a text to appeal to; perhaps one with the date

of the publication and the name of the author; perhaps one with additional pieces of information more or less illustrative of the history of the drama. There is, in short, something like documentary evidence, much or little as the case may be. When, however, an actor returns with his experience the case is widely different. He talks over what he has learnt. He may communicate a piece of professional information to one friend which he conceals from another. He may give the character of a play in which he has taken a part by instalments; or his own *rôle*, with the full amount of detail (perhaps word for word) from first to last; but of the *rôles* of others only a general view. He may speak of an incident or a scene as having been effective on such or such an occasion, without giving the whole of the circumstances which made it so ; and such an incident may thus get transplanted or inserted into a drama with which it had originally no connection. Finally, a state of things like that which we have just described would leave posterity much to learn. There might be any amount of borrowing, reproduction, or adaptation, the evidence of which would rest not on definite texts, either in print or manuscripts, but on imperfect biographical notices, uncertain inferences, or traditions, of which the value was unknown.

Such was the stage in Germany.

Let us now turn to England, with a special view to the date and authorship of the earliest English drama on the story of Hamlet ; and, moreover, with a clear understanding that the first English play of Hamlet is not necessarily a play by Shakespear. It may be so or it may not, and upon this point there is room for a great difference of opinion.

Of a "Hamlet," undoubtedly Shakespearian, and as a printed play, the earliest date is A.D. 1603. Of this edition only two copies are known—one in the library of the Duke of Devonshire, and one in the British Museum. As, however, there is a reprint of it in Hallwell's, and another in the Cambridge edition of Shakespear, we have four means of comparing with the later texts. From these it differs notably, and that on the side of defectiveness.

Then follows the fuller, and probably more authentic edition of the following year—the Quarto of A.D. 1604.

Here, then, are not only two editions of a "Hamlet," but two editions of a "Hamlet" of undoubted Shakespearian authorship. With the composition which now comes under notice, and which is really the oldest recorded drama on the subject of the Prince of Denmark, the case is widely different. The work itself has long been known—only however by name; inasmuch as no copy of the play, either in print or manuscript, has come down to us, nor have any fragments of it been preserved. Indeed there is no evidence that it was ever printed. We know, however, that it contained a ghost—perhaps we should say *the* ghost. There is nothing which connects it with the name of Shakespear, nothing which assigns it to any one else. We know, however, the date—A.D. 1589; so that if written by Shakespear it would have been written by him in his twenty-third year. This calculation we must check by an enquiry as to Shakespear's life during this interval, and we shall do well in beginning earlier than the important year 1589. To know what he was doing then we must know what he had been doing before. There is not much that is very clear for this period. He was baptized April 26, 1564, and there are fair reasons for believing that his baptism was only a few days later than his birth; so that we may safely say that '64 was the date of his birth and baptism.

By '84 he was the father of a daughter, and two sons (twins) who were born in Stratford. He was now in his twentieth year.

What he did immediately after this is uncertain, and by '90 (*anno ætatis*, 26) he was not only in London, but the joint manager of the theatre at the Blackfriars. He began as an actor, but he was probably this and something more—a writer who put the older and ruder dramas submitted to his judgment into a more modern and less uncouth form and style. He did this (as he also acted) for some time and afterwards. At any rate, he was in 1589 an actor and manager, rather than a single-handed dramatist. How early he began to be this is uncertain; probably soon after the time of leaving Stratford, which was soon after the birth of the twins.

In '91 was published Spenser's " Tears of the Muses," in which there is a *supposed* allusion to Shakespear; in which he is believed to be indicated by the name *Willy*.

In '92 Robert Greene died. Now Robert Greene was one of what we should now call a *clique*, of which Marlow (who was born in the same year as Shakespear), Peele (somewhat older), and Nash were members. Greene was a clergyman, and with less poetry or rhetoric than his fellows, was, from his miscellaneous and discursive reading, a very useful man in the coterie. He wrote poems and plays. But he was, also, a translator, among other languages, from the Spanish. As the romances thus translated often gave the plot to plays, such a man is prominent in the history of dramatic literature. He had lived, with his companions (one of whom was the unhappy genius Marlow), a dissolute life, and in his last days left to the world a sort of legacy in the shape of a warning. His "Groat's Worth of Rest Purchased by a Million of Repentance " is addressed to his fellow-workmen. Let them mend their ways: let them eschew, among others, one "Johannes Factotum," one who has a "tiger's heart in a player's hide;" one who, plagiarist as he was, and enriched by the work of other men, thought himself the only Shake-scene in the company. The import of this puerile quibble is manifest; or should any doubt of its application remain, a publication of the next year dispels it.

Greene's work was posthumous. Its editor was Chettle. Now in '93 Chettle makes, in his "Kind-hart's Dream," amends or apology to Shakespear. Greene was a friend of Marlow's, and Marlow's dissipation and religion had shocked him (Chettle).

From this we learn that, in his twenty-ninth year, Shakespear had become of sufficient prominence to be sneered at by one of his older contemporaries— the *Vorschule* or *Foreschool*, as it is called in Germany, of Shakespear.

In the same year with Chettle's "Kind-hart's Dream " is published Shakespear's " Venus and Adonis," a *non*-dramatic poem. This he dedicates to the Earl of Sonthampton as the " first heir of invention." In an ordinary subject, and in ordinary times, these words would make the "Venus and Adonis" Shakespear's first work. But with a manager of a theatre a great deal of unrecognized work, in the way of the modification, the adoption, and the improvement of other men's dramas, may have to be done; and in this way, doubtless, Shakespear had done much.

In '94 his "Rape of Lucrece" is published. Still there is nothing in the shape of a separate substantive drama connected with the name of Shakespear; and this is five years after the date of the "Hamlet" to which Nash alludes. In this year Spenser, in his "Colin Clout's Come Home Again," alludes to Shakespear unambiguously.

By the end of '97 (Shakespear is now 33) "Richard II.," "Richard III.," and "Romeo and Juliet" are *published*.

Before the end of '98, not less than fifteen plays may be assigned to Shakespear. From Ames' list we get the "Two Gentlemen of Verona," "Love's Labour Lost," "Love's Labour Won" (which, as first suggested by Dr. Farmer, seems to have the original title of "All's Well that Ends Well"), "Midsummer Night's Dream," "Merchant of Venice," "Richard II.," "Richard III.," "Henry IV.," "King John," "Titus Andronicus," and "Romeo and Juliet." The evidence of the identity of "All's Well that Ends Well" with "Love's Labour Won" is capable of being improved; indeed, it is merely a guess, though a probable and ingenious one. "Henry IV." is presumed to mean the two parts. If so, the number in Ames is twelve, a number which coincides very closely with the list which we should have got from other quarters — such as allusions to the " Comedy of Errors," and the actual publication of " Romeo and Juliet " and the two " Richards." The only drama, indeed, which, on the strength of evidence *aliunde*, can be added to the enumeration is Henry VI. ;" which, with its three parts, brings up the number to fifteen. Nevertheless, Ames' dramas look like selected examples, or specimens of Shakespear's best works, rather than as a list of the whole of them. In any case, however, the omission of " Hamlet," if it were then in existence, and known to be a work of Shakespear's, is remarkable.

In 1599 he published the non-dramatic poem entitled " The Passionate Pilgrim ; " and this brings us as near the date of the Hamlet of 1603 as we can be brought.

I now submit that, though the " Hamlet " of 1598 may have no existence *verbatim et literatim* in its original language, it may be either wholly or partially preserved, or at least adequately represented, by a translation in another language ; that language being the German, and the text that of the *Bestrafte Brudermord.*

This is at variance with the general, and, as I believe, the universal opinion, and the reasons in favour of the view, so far as they are independent of text, to which the reader is referred, I will now produce. In respect to the external form of the play the differences are very considerable ; though as far as the sequence of the scenes are concerned, and the general character of the framework of the dialogue, the agreement is of the closest.

There is a Prologue, in which Night addresses the
Three Fairies. It is in verse, the body of the play
being in prose. Herein Night tells the Sisters that
while she is speaking a great crime is going on—viz.,
the wicked and incestuous marriage of the murderous,
adulterous, and usurping brother of Hamlet's father.
In this Prologue one of the German commentators
sees a nearer approach to poetry than is to be found
elsewhere; and so far as it is poetical, it is, or may
be, Shakespearian.

Then come the Dramatis Personæ. Here the
order is more ancient than modern, the males and
females being mixed together, instead of the females
being arranged by themselves at the end of the list;
and the order being less regulated by the rank of the
interlocutors than by the order in which they appear
on the stage; though this is not adhered to with the
strictness of the classical drama.

The names, too, are different, and Polonius and
Reynaldo are Corambus and Montalto, as in the
"Hamlet" of A.D. 1603. More remarkable still are the
names of Hamlet's mother and uncle. The mother
is called Signe—evidently a name of Scandinavian
origin, the most famous Norse love-tale being that of
Signe[15] and Hagbart; whose sad fate made their
names household words to every youth and maiden
of the North. The story is alluded to in the most
popular Swedish poem of our own day; for it is pre-
eminently the subject which an old minstrel would
be supposed to take up when he changed his hand
from records of savagery and heroism to those connected with the more tender passions :—

A minstrel sat beside the throne, he sang his best that day,

[15] I write *Signe* for *Sigrie meo periculo.*

And told a tale of tenderness, an old Norwegian lay ;
Of Hacbart's fate and *Signe's* love—his voice was sweet and
   low,
That iron hearts began to melt, and tears were seen to flow.
Frithiof's Saga, xvii.

The uncle's name is Eric. This has undoubtedly
at the first view as Scandinavian a look as Signe ; but
it is English as well. In the tale already noticed, of
Argentile and Curan, the hero has a wicked uncle,
and, just as it is in the present play, Eric is his name.
But in both the romances from which the poem
seems most especially to be taken no such name is
found ; the usurper there being . . . . Without
enlarging upon the extent to which this connects
Warner's (Havelok) Cuaran with Shakespear's
"Hamlet," we may fairly infer that some lost tradition
or some unknown record is the common foundation
for the two names. Individually, I go further, and
think either it may have had a Latin title—*Gesta
Erici* (or *Eorici*) *Regis;* or, that out of confusion
both of title and subject the actual *Chronicon Regis
Erici* may have been so called. The assumed confusion, however, goes farther, until *Gesta Regis* ends
in the *King's Jester*, and *Eric* becomes *Yorick*. It
is only, however, in Shakespear that the Jester's
name appears ; indeed, in the German " Hamlet," the
whole scene of the grave-diggers is conspicuous for
its absence.

How this name originated is probably to be found
in the history of Anlaf Cwiran, and notices of him in
the Anglo-Saxon Chronicle.[16] When Anlaf was driven
out of his kingdom, the Northumbrians chose *Eric*,
the son of Harald, in his stead ; Harold meaning
either Harald Haarfager or Harold Bluetooth.

[16] See page 34.

The scene changes whenever a new speaker enters. Here we may turn to " Titus Andronicus." It has no Prologue; neither are there Scenes, or rather the scenes, to the amount of ten, are called Acts.

The Dramatis Personæ in the English Play are:—

SATURNINUS, *son to the late Emperor* of Rome.
BASSIANUS, *brother to* Saturninus.
TITUS ANDRONICUS, a noble Roman.
MARCUS ANDRONICUS, brother to Titus.

LUCIUS,
QUINTUS, } *sons to* Titus Andronicus.
MARTIUS,
MUTIUS,

Young LUCIUS, *a boy, son to* Lucius.
PUBLICIS, *son to* Marcus, *the Tribune.*
ÆMILIUS, *a noble* Roman.

ALARBUS,
CHIRON, } *sons to* Tamora.
DEMETRIUS,

AARON, a Moor.
A Captain, Tribune, Messenger and Clown.
Goths *and* Romans.
TAMORA, *Queen of the* Goths.
LAVINIA, *daughter to* Titus Andronicus.
A Nurse and a Black Child.
Kinsmen of Titus, *Senators, Tribunes.*
Soldiers and Attendants.

In the German "Titus Andronicus:"—

VESPASIAN.
The Roman Keyser.
TITUS ANDRONICUS.
ANDRONICA.

Æthiopessa, *Queen of* Æthiopia.
Morian (*i.e.*, Aaron the Moor).
Helicates, eldest son of Æthiopessa.
Consort of Andronicus.
Victonades.
. *Messengers, White Guards.*

With the exception of "Titus Andronicus," all the
six plays in Cohn's valuable work are provided with
a preliminary notice ; telling us what is known about
the date of their representation. Of Andronicus we
are merely informed that it was acted about A.D.
1600, and that it was printed A.D. 1620, and reprinted
A.D. 1624. Now A.D. 1600 is very early for a play of
Shakespear's to reappear in Germany; though it
must be added that, from a well-known passage from
Meres, we learn not only that a play with such a
title was acted in England, but also attributed to
Shakespear. The time, then, is not too short for a
simple transfer. It is very short, however, for such
a transformation of Dramatis Personæ, and such a
change in the character of the scenes, as the German
play presents. Natural degradation, corruption, or
whatever we choose to call it, is well-nigh out of the
question. If the change be real it must be referred
to a process of conscious adaptation ; and of this
there is a notable sign in the name of "The Roman
Keyser," and in one of his speeches. In the stage
directions he is described as the " Keyser who is not
yet Keyser ; " which is very nearly, in *Latin,* for
the " Cæsar who is not Augustus." But in the
dialogue he salutes Andronicus as Emperor—*i.e.*, in
German, as Keyser ; and again, says " Shall I, who
am Cæsar, not be Emperor." This is German to all

intents and purposes. Adaptation, however, is not the only process which accounts for it. The play may have been German from the beginning.

The other complications, however, which arise from the agreement between the German "Hamlet" and the German "Titus Andronicus," are too numerous to be allowed to detain us. The reason for alluding to the present one lies in the argument it supplies against the doctrine of the difference between the nobler English texts and the more ignoble German ones being due to wear and tear, to time, to degradation, to vulgarization, and the like; though between the two "Titi Andronici" the difference between the better and the worse is of the smallest; not to mention the doubts as to the shares which Shakespear had in the English one.

These are arguments derived from the general character of the play in respect to its outward form. The special points of detail that supply any are the following three : —

1. The blunder about Roscius.
2. The allusion of Juvenal.
3. The reference to Portugal.

This last is of more weight than the other two two combined.

1. THE BLUNDER ABOUT ROSCIUS.

From the English Hamlet.

Polonius.—My lord, I have news to tell you.

Hamlet.—My lord, I have news to tell you. When *Roscius* was an actor in Rome—

Polonius. The actors are coming hither, my lord.

Hamlet. Buz, Buz !

Polonius. Upon mine honour—

Hamlet. " Then came each actor on his ass "—

Polonius. The best actors in the world, either for tragedy, comedy, history, &c.—Act ii. Scene ii.

From the German Hamlet.

Corambus. News, news ! my lord. I have news to tell you. The actors are come, my lord.

Hamlet. When *Marius Roscius* was an actor at Rome, what fine times those were.

Corambus. Ha, ha, ha ! How you always do laugh at me, my lord !

Hamlet. O! Jephthah, Jephthah ! what a fair daughter hast thou !

Corambus. Why, my lord, you are still harping on my daughter.

Hamlet. Well, well, old greybeard, let the master of the actors come in.

Corambus. I will, my lord.—Act ii. Scene vi.

This is from the translation. In the original German *Marius Roscius* is *Marus Russig. Roscius*, however, is doubtless the true word. But what means *Marus?* It is submitted that it means *Amerinus.* Now there were two *Roscii*, and Cicero delivered an oration in defence of both. One was Roscius the actor; the other, *Sextus* Roscius *Amerinus*, who was no actor at all. This, however, is the Roscius of Corambus. Now this is a blunder that requires as much scholarship to achieve as to avoid ; being one that a learned man might make from inadvertency whereas an unlearned one could not make it at all. It was certainly *not* made by Shakespear. This we

H

know from his text, where *Roscius* stands alone. It could scarcely have been made by the supposed adapters who came after him.

2. THE ALLUSION TO *Juvenal.*

This is in the same predicament with the preceding. It is more classical than the text of the supposed original.

From the English Hamlet.

Osric. Sweet lord, if your friendship were at leisure, I should impart a thing to you from his Majesty.

Hamlet. I will receive it with all diligence of spirit; put your bonnet to its right use; 'tis for the head.

Osric. I thank your lordship, 'tis very hot.

Hamlet. No, believe me, 'tis very cold; the wind is northerly.

Osric. It is indifferent cold, my lord, indeed.

Hamlet. Methinks it is very sultry, and hot, for my complexion.

Osric. Exceedingly, my lord; it is very sultry—as 't were —I cannot tell how, etc.—ACT v. SCENE ii.

From the German Hamlet.

Hamlet. Look, Horatio, this fool is infinitely dearer to the King than my poor person. Let's hear what he has to say.

Phantasmo. Welcome to home, Prince Hamlet! Have you heard the last news? The King has laid a wager on you and young Leonardo. You are to measure your skill at fencing, and he who gives his opponent the first two thrusts is to win a white Neapolitan horse.

Hamlet. Are you sure of what you say?

Phantasmo. Ay, ay, so it is, as I say.

Hamlet. Horatio, what may this mean ? I and Leonardo to fight. They have been imposing on this poor fool, for one can make him believe what one likes. Observe ; Signor Phantasmo, 'tis horribly cold.

Phantasmo. Ay, ay, 'tis horribly cold.

[*His teeth chattering with cold.*

Hamlet. Now it is no more cold.

Phantasmo. You're right, my lord, just the happy medium.

Hamlet. But now it is very hot.

[*Wiping his face.*

Phantasmo. O what a dreadful heat !

[*Also wiping away the perspiration.*

Hamlet. It seems to me 'tis neither very cold nor very warm.

Phantasmo. Yes, now it is just temperate.

Hamlet. Do you see, Horatio, one can make him believe what one will. Phantasmo, go, get thee to the King, and say I'll wait upon him instantly.

With this compare—

Natio comæda est. Rides ? Meliore cachinno
Concutitur ; flet si lacrymas conspexit amici,
Nec dolet ; igniculum brumæ si tempore poscas,
Accipit endromiden ; si dixeris " Æstuo," sudat.

JUV. SAT. iii. v. 100—103.

This is what the satirist says of the Greek para site. In the German text there is, to say the least, a similarity sufficient to suggest a comparison. The English text has never suggested anything; not even to Johnson, who had paraphrased the satire.

THE REFERENCE TO PORTUGAL.

From the English Hamlet.

Hamlet. How long hast thou been a grave-maker ?

First Clown. Of all the days in the year, I came to it that day that our last King Hamlet o'ercame Fortinbras.

Hamlet. How long is that since?

First Clown. Cannot you tell that? Every fool can tell that. It was the very day that young Hamlet was born—he that was mad and sent into England?

Hamlet. Ay, marry, why was he sent into England.

First Clown. Why, because he was mad. He shall recover his wits there; or, if he do not, it's no great matter there.

Hamlet. Why?

First Clown. 'Twill not be seen there in him; there are men as mad as he.—ACT V. SCENE i.

From the German Hamlet.

King. We have determined to send you to England, because the crown is friendly to our own, as if to refresh yourself there for a time, because the air is wholesomer, and may better promote your recovery. We will give you some of our own attendants, who shall accompany you, and serve you faithfully.

Hamlet. Ay, ay, King, send me off to *Portugal, that I may never come back again*, that is the best plan.

King. No, *not to Portugal but to England*, and those two shall accompany you on the journey. But when you arrive in England, you shall have more attendants.—iii. 10.

Now if the older Hamlet (or the Hamlet with the older allusion) were connected with any other date but that of the year 1598, I should account for the text by supposing that it applied to the King of that country, Don Sebastian; whose unfortunate expedition into Africa ended with the Battle of Alcazar. Here he was thoroughly defeated by Abdelmelek, King of Morocco; but, as his body was not found on the field. and as he never afterwards appeared alive, his fate has remained a mystery from that time to this. His subjects, to the very last, expected his re-appearance, and long after the natural date of his death there were sanguine Portuguese who believed that, like Arthur in Avalon, he was sleeping a long, perhaps an endless, sleep in the Canary Islands; a belief which is said to be not even now wholly extinct.

The fate of Don Sebastian affected the imagination of men all over Europe, and nowhere more than in England; and in England it gave birth to a play by Peele—"The Battle of Alcazar." An historical event will keep longer than a passing allusion. It also crops out again in the reign of King James I.; but this was under circumstances well exhibited by Colonel Cunningham in his remarks of Massinger's play, " Believe as you List." It was acted about the time of the negotiations of the famous Spanish marriage ; and as allusions to the fate of Don Sebastian were unpleasant to the Spanish Court, an allusion in Mas-singer's play (or one reasonably supposed to be such) is forbidden by the dramatic censor of the time.

Still the allusion is a possible one, just as the stanzas of the present Laureate on the " Balaclava Charge " might be written in the present year. The subject, however, in either case would be an old one. In 1598, however, the converse was the case. Indeed the most plausible objection to that date is the pos-sible one of its being too new; for it falls within the very year to which the older Hamlet, *as its latest date*. As Peele wrote on both expeditions—Don Sebastian's and the one under notice, we find, as we expect from the high character of the editor, ample information as to each of them, in Mr. Dyce's edition of that poet's works, from which the following notice is an extract;—

"In 1589, while the public exultation at the defeat of the Spanish Armada had not yet subsided, a band of gallant adventurers (chiefly excited by the desire of gain or glory) fitted out, almost entirely at their own expense, a fleet for an expedition into Portugal, for the declared purpose of setting on the throne of that country the bastard Don Antonio, who had taken refuge in England. On the 18th of April the armament set sail from Plymouth, consisting of 180 vessels and 21,000 men under the command of Sir Francis Drake and Sir John Norris. A minute detail of the disasters that ensued would here be out of place. Suffice it to say that about eleven thousand persons perished in this expedition, and of the eleven hundred gentlemen who accompanied it, only three hundred and fifty returned to their native country.—*Works of T. Peele, edited by J. Dyce*, p. 540.

Peele's works on the two expeditions are three in number : *two* being on this. The "Farewell" comes at the beginning; the "Eclogue Gratulatory" at the conclusion of it. To the "Farewell" is annexed "A Tale of Troy," written as stimulus to his countrymen that they "may march in equipage of honour and arms with their glorious and renowned predecessors, the Trojans." Here we get the following allusion to the hero of Alcazar—it may be added, the hero of Peele's own play on that event:—

> Bid theatres and proud tragedians,
> Bid Mahomet, Scipio, and mighty Tambarlaine,
> King Charlemagne, *Tom Stukely*, and the rest,
>   Adieu.

The "Eclogue Gratulatory" is dedicated to the

Earl of Essex, who had joined the expedition, and was, moreover, one of the few who came back from it.

Eclogue Gratulatory.

Piers.

Certes, sir shepherd, comen he is from far,
From wrath of deepest seas and storm of war,
Safe is he come.   O, swell, my pipe, with joy,
To the old buildings of new-reared Troy.

Io, io, pæan!

From sea, from shore, where he with swink and sweat,
Felt foeman's rage and summer's parching heat,
Safe is he come, laden with honour's spoil,
O, swell, my pipe, with joy, and break the while.

Io, io, pæan!

Palinode.

Thou foolish swain that thus art overjoy'd,
How soon may here thy courage be accoy'd!
If he be one come new from western coast,
Small cause has he, or those, for him to boast.

I see no palm, I see no laurel boughs
Circle his temples or adorn his brows;
I hear no triumph for this late return,
But many a herdsman more disposed to mourn.

The scene from which this Notice of Portugal is taken, is one where the dialogue is between Hamlet and his father, in the middle of the play, the remark upon the madness of the English being towards the end of it; the grave-diggers and the name of Yorick being wholly non-existent in the German.

In respect to the allusion to Juvenal, it is probable that the "wiping of the face" re-appears in the handkerchief which his mother lends him during the fencing match.

Taking these three special points as we find them, it is submitted that the third is in favour of the German Hamlet dating from the year in question, and the other two are more against than in favour of Shakespear having been the author of the play. The remainder of the argument is less open to isolated points of evidence. It lies in the text itself, upon which the reader must form his own judgment.

ON THE DOUBLE PERSONALITY OF THE HAMLET OF SAXO GRAMMATICUS—THE HAMLET OF SHAKESPEAR—ITS RELATION TO THE GERMAN HAMLET.

BY DR. R. G. LATHAM, M.A., M.D., ETC.

PART II.

In the following translation there is no attempt whatever at anything like a reproduction of the language of Shakespear's time; still less is there any use of Shakespear's own language. With the version in Cohn's "Shakespear in Germany," which may be read, side by side, with the original, the translator has acted differently; and where a German word is, without much violence, capable of being rendered by the corresponding word in Shakespear he has so rendered it. Thus, in a well-known line the German runs "our memory is yet *fresh (frische)*." Shakespear has "*green.*" So has the translator; and, from his point of view, viz:—that the German play was founded on the English, the licence is legitimate. From a point of view, however, diametrically opposite, no such licence is allowed; indeed, there is no temptation to indulge in it.

In the way of language, the German of the text seems to be the German of the time of the last owner but one of the manuscript, rather than that of the date of the original translation. An allusion, also,

I

to certain *actresses* (in Act ii.—Scene vii.) seems to have been " foisted in by the players," and the gallantries of the King of Saxony to be alluded to. So far, then, as these two points are concerned, the principle (otherwise sound) that " nothing is older than its newest part " must be abated. The numerous Gallicisms which help us to fix the date of the language are inserted between parentheses and italicized.

TRAGŒDIA.

DER BESTRAFTE BRUDERMORD

ODER

PRINZ HAMLET AUS * DÄNNEMARK.

PERSONS REPRESENTED.

1.—*In the Prologue.*

NIGHT, *in a car covered with stars.*
ALECTO.
THISIPHONE.
MEGÄRA.

2.—*In the Tragedy.*

GHOST *of the old King of Denmark.*
†ERICO, *brother to the King.*
HAMLET, *Prince (son) of the murdered King.*

---

* The date of the MS. is October, 1710. It came into the possession of Conrad Ekhof, of Gotha, who died June 16, 1778. In 1781 the full text is found in the periodical *Olla Podrida*. Berlin. Part II., pp. 18–68. This is the text of Cohn's impression. This applies to the date of the text only. For the date of the earlier representations, see pp. 147, 148.

† See p. 145.

SIGRIE, (*sic*, ? SIGNE) *the Queen, Hamlet's mother.*
HORATIO, *a noble friend of the Prince.*
CORAMBUS, *Royal Chamberlain.*
LEONHARDUS, *his son.*
OPHELIA, *his daughter.*
PHANTASMO, *the Court fool.*
FRANCISCO, *Officer of the Guard.*
JENS, *a clown.*
CARL, *the principal of the Actors.*
Corporal of the Guard.
Two speaking Ruffians (Zwei redende Banditen).
Two Sentinels.
Life Guards,
Servants of the Court, } *Mute (stumme).*
Two Actors,

PROLOGUE.

I am the dim Night which sends all things to sleep,
I am the wife of Morpheus, the time for vicious pastime,
I am the guardian of the thieves, and the protection of those
    in love;
I am the dim Night and have it in my power
To practice evil, to sadden men.
My mantle covers the shame and rest of the harlot.
Before Phœbus shall shine I will begin a game.
You, children of my breast, and daughters of my lust,
You, Furies, up—up, forward, show yourselves !
Come, listen attentively, as to what will soon take place.

Alecto.

What says the dim Night, the queen of silence;
What new work does she propose,—what is her will and
    pleasure ?

Megära.

From Acheron's dark pit come I, Mägera, hither,
From thee, thou mother of evil, to hear thy desire.

Tisiphone.

And I, Tisiphone,—what you have to say, say ;
Thou black Hecate, whether I can serve thee.

Night.

Listen, ye Furies all three, ye children of darkness and
bearers of misfortune ; listen to your happy-crowned Queen
of the Night, the patroness of thieves and robbers, the
friend and light of the incendiary, the lover of stolen goods,
the Goddess dear above all others to the adulterous,—how
often are my altars honoured by them ! During this night
and the coming morrow must ye stand by me, for it is the
King of this land that burns with love of his brother's
wife, and has for her sake, murdered him, that he may
possess both her and the kingdom. Now is the time that
they lie together. I will throw my mantle over them so that
neither may see their sin. Therefore be ready to sow the
seeds of disunion, mingle poison with their marriage, and
jealousy with their hearts' blood. Kindle a fire of revenge,
and let the sparks fly over the whole realm ; confound the
blood of kinsmen in the net of crime, and comfort Hell,
whereby those who swim in the sea of murder may soon
drown. Fly, speed, fulfil my commands.

Thisiphone.

I have already heard enough, and will soon make good
More than the dim Night can of herself imagine.

Megära.

Pluto's own self shall not put into my mind
So much as, within a short time, ye shall experience from
    me.

Alecto.

I fan the sparks and make the fire burn :
I will, before it first dawns, break to bits the whole game.

Night.

Hasten, then, and, while I am ascending, make good your
*   * course.

[*Ascends. Music.*

ACT I.

SCENE I.

Sentinels.

First Sentinel. Who's there ?
Second Sentinel. A friend.
First Sentinel. What friend ?
Second Sentinel. Sentinel.
First Sentinel. O ho, comrade !—you're come to relieve
me. I wish the time may not be so long to you as it has
been to me.
Second Sentinel. Oh, comrade, it is not so cold now.
First Sentinel. Cold or not, I've a Hell's own sweat.
Second Sentinel. Why so timoursome ?—that's not suit-
able to a soldier. He must fear neither friend nor foe ; nor
even the Devil himself.

---

* The following lines, which give the opening speech of Night in
the original, may serve as a specimen of the metre. Night's second
speech is in prose.

Ich bin die dunkle Nacht, die alles schlafend macht,
Ich bin des Morpheus Weib, der Laster Zeitvertreib,
Ich bin der Diebe Schutz, und der Verliebten Trutz,
Ich bin die dunkle Nacht, und hab' in meiner Macht,
Die Bosheit auszuüben, die Menschen zu betrüben,
Mein Mantel decket zu der Huren Schand' und Ruh',
Eh' Phöbus noch wird prangen, will ich ein Spiel anfangen.
Ihr Kinder meiner Brust, ihr Töchter meiner Lust,
Ihr Furien, auf! auf! hervor und lasst euch sehen,
Kommt, höret fleissig zu, was kurzens soll geschehen.

First Sentinel. It's all very well; but let him once catch you behind, and you'll be taught to sing *Miserere Domine.*

Second Sentinel. What, then, is it that has really frightened you?

First Sentinel. I'll tell you. I've seen a ghost in the front of the castle, and he has twice tried to pitch me down from the bastion.

Second Sentinel. Shut up you fool. Dead dogs don't bite. I'll see whether a ghost that has neither flesh nor blood can hurt me.

First Sentinel. Well; if he do shew himself, see what he will be like, and whether or no he gives you trouble. I'll to the watch-house. Adieu.

Second Sentinel. Only be off; perhaps you were born on a Sunday, and can see ghosts of all sorts. I'll now mount guard.

    [*Healths, to the sound of trumpets within.*

Second Sentinel. Our new King makes merry. They are drinking healths.

SCENE II.

(*Ghost of the King, steps, approaches the Sentinel, and frightens him*).

Second Sentinel. O! Saint Anthony of Padua, stand by me. Now I *do* see what my comrade told me. O, Saint Velten; if only my first round were over I'd run away like a rogue.

    [*Trumpets and drums within.*

Second Sentinel. I wish I'd a draught of wine from the King's table.

    [*Ghost from behind gives him a box on
     the ear, and he drops his musket.*

Second Sentinel. There's the Devil himself on the game. I'm so frightened that I cannot move from the spot.

SCENE III.

Horatio, Soldiers.

Second Sentinel. Who's there?

Horatio. The Rounds.

Second Sentinel. Which.

Horatio. Main Round.

Second Sentinel. Stand Watch. Corporal forward. Shoulder arms.

> [*Francisco and Watch come out and give the word from the other side.*

Horatio. Sentinel, look well to your post; the Prince himself may, perhaps, go the rounds (*patrolliren*). Be caught sleeping and it may cost you your head.

Second Sentinel. I wish the whole company were here. Not a man of them would go to sleep; and I must either be relieved, or run away, and then, to-morrow, be hanged on the highest gallows.

Horatio. Why?

Second Sentinel. Oh, my lord, there's a ghost here, which appears every quarter of an hour; it has so put me out of sorts that I could fancy myself a live man in Purgatory.

Francisco. This is just what the sentinel last relieved has told me.

Second Sentinel. Aye, aye; only stop a bit. It won't keep away long.

> [*Ghost passes across the stage.*

Horatio. On my life it is a ghost, and looks just like the late King of Denmark.

Francisco. He bears himself sadly, and seems as if he would fain say something.

Horatio. There is some mystery in this.

SCENE IV.

Hamlet.

Second Sentinel. Who's there?

Hamlet. Hush!

Second Sentinel. Who's there ?

Hamlet. Hush !

Second Sentinel. Answer, or I'll teach you better manners.

Hamlet. A friend.

Second Sentinel. What friend ?

Hamlet. Friend to the kingdom.

Francisco. By my life it is the Prince.

Horatio. Your Highness,—is it you or not ?

Hamlet. What ! you here, Horatio ?   What brings you ?

Horatio. Yonr Highness, I have gone the rounds to see that every one is at his post.

Hamlet. That's like an honest soldier ; for on you rests the safety of the King and kingdom.

Horatio. Your Highness, a strange thing has happened. Regularly every quarter of an hour a ghost appears ; and, to my mind, he is very like the late King—your father. He frightens the sentinels terribly.

Hamlet. I hope not, for the souls of the good rest quietly till the time of their resurrection.

Horatio. Yet, so it is.   I've seen it myself.

Francisco. And he has frightened me, Your Highness.

Second Sentinel. And he has given me a good box on the ear.

Hamlet. What is the time ?

Francisco. Midnight.

Hamlet. Good !—it is just the time when ghosts, when they *do* walk, show themselves.

[*Healths again.*

Hamlet. Holloa !—what is this ?

Horatio. I fancy it is the Court, still at the health-drinking.

Hamlet. Right, Horatio !   My Lord and father and uncle makes himself merry with his followers (*adhærenten*).   Alas, Horatio ! I know not how it is that since my father's death I am always so sick at heart ; while my royal mother has already forgotten him, and the King still sooner ; for while I was in Germany he had himself crowned with all haste in

Denmark. But for some sort of show of right he has made over to me the Crown of Norway, and appealed to the will of the States.

Ghost and others.

Second Sentinel. O, dear!—here's the ghost again.

Horatio. Does Your Highness see now?

Francisco. Don't be frightened, Your Highness.

　　　　[*Ghost crosses the stage and beckons to Hamlet.*

Hamlet. The Ghost beckons me. Gentlemen, stand aside awhile. Horatio, do not go far away from here. I will follow the ghost and know what he wants.

　　　　　　　　　　　　　　　　　　[*Exit.*

Horatio. Gentlemen! let us follow him to see that he take no harm.

　　　　　　　　　　　　　　　　[*Exeunt.*

　　　　[*Ghost beckons Hamlet to the middle of the*
　　　　　　stage and opens his jaws several times.

Hamlet. Speak! say who thou art, and what thou desirest.

Ghost. Hamlet.

Hamlet. Sir.

Ghost. Hamlet.

Hamlet. What desirest thou?

Ghost. Hear me, Hamlet, for the time approaches when I must give myself back to the place whence I have come. Hear and give heed to what I shall relate.

Hamlet. Speak, thou departed shade of my royal Lord and father.

Ghost. Then hear. Son Hamlet, what I have to tell you is thy father's unnatural death.

Hamlet. What! unnatural death!

Ghost. Ay! unnatural death! Know that I had the habit to which nature had accustomed me to go in my royal pleasure-garden every day after my noontide meal, and there to take an hour's rest. One day when I did this came my brother, thirsting for my crown, and had with him the subtile (*subtilen*) juice of ebenon (*ebeno*).   This oil, or juice, has the following effect :—As soon as a few drops of it mix with the blood of a man, they, immediate, clog the passages of life (*Lebensadern*) and destroy life.   This juice did he, while I was sleeping, pour into my ear ; and as soon as ever it reached my head, I could not but die at once ; whereupon it was given out that I had died of a violent apoplexy.   So was I of my kingdom, my wife, and my life robbed by this tyrant.

Hamlet. Just heavens ! if this be true I swear to revenge you.

Ghost. I cannot rest until my unnatural murder be revenged.

[*Exit.*

Hamlet. I swear that I will not rest until I have had my revenge on this fratricide.

SCENE VI.

Horatio, Hamlet, Francisco.

Horatio. How is it with Your Highness ? Why so terror-stricken ?   Hast thou perchance been disturbed (*alterirt*) ?

Hamlet. Yes, verily ; beyond all measure.

Horatio. Has Your Highness seen the Ghost ?

Hamlet. Aye ! truly—seen and spoken to it.

Horatio. O, Heavens ! this bodes something strange.

Hamlet. He has revealed to me a horrible thing ; therefore I pray you, gentlemen, stand by me in a matter that calls for vengeance.

Horatio. You are surely convinced of my faithfulness, only tell me.

Francisco. Your Highness cannot doubt as to my help.

Hamlet. Gentlemen, before I reveal the matter you must swear an oath on your truth and honour.

Francisco. Your Highness knows the love I bear you. I will willingly risk my life if only you can have your revenge.

Horatio. Put thou the oath to us, and we will stand by you as true men.

Hamlet. Then, lay your finger on my sword.—" We swear."

Horatio and Francisco. We swear.

Ghost (within). We swear.

Hamlet. Holla!—what is this? Swear again.

Horatio and Francisco. We swear.

Ghost. We swear.

Hamlet. This means something strange. Come, once more, and let us go to the other side. We swear.

Horatio and Francisco. We swear.

Ghost. We swear.

Hamlet. What is this? It is an echo which sends back to the rebound of our own words. Come, we will go to another spot. We swear.

Hamlet. O! I now hear what this means. It seems that the Ghost of my father is displeased at my making the matter known. Gentlemen, I pray you, leave me; to-morrow I will reveal everything.

Horatio and Francisco. Farewell, Your Highness.

[*Exit Francisco.*

Hamlet. Horatio come hither.

Horatio. What is Your Highness' will?

Hamlet. Has the other gone?

Horatio. He has.

Hamlet. I know, Horatio, that thou hast at all times been true to me, so I will reveal to you what the Ghost has told me, namely :—that my father died a violent death. My father, he who is now my father, has murdered him.

Horatio. O heaven! what do I hear?

Hamlet. Thou knowest, O Horatio, that my dear departed father was wont every day after his noontide meal to sleep an hour in his summer-house. The villain, knowing this, comes to my father and pours into his ear, whilst he is asleep, the juice of ebenon, under which poison my father gave up the ghost. This the accursed dog did in order to obtain the crown; but from this moment I will put on an affected madness, and in my affectation so skilfully play my part that I shall find an opportunity to avenge my father's death.

Horatio. If so it is to be, I pledge myself to be true to Your Highness.

Hamlet. Horatio, I will so avenge myself on this ambitious and adulterous murderer that posterity shall speak of it till eternity. I will now go and dissemble and bide my time until I find an opportunity to effect my revenge.

[*Exeunt.*

SCENE VII.

(King, Queen, Hamlet, Corambus, and Court).

King. Although our royal brother's death is still fresh in the memory of us all, and it befits us to suspend all state-shows, we must, nevertheless, change our mourning suits into crimson, purple, and scarlet, since my late departed brother's relic has now become our dearest consort. Let, then, every one shew himself cheerful, and make himself a sharer of our mirth. But do you, Prince Hamlet, do the like. See how your Lady mother is grieved and troubled at your melancholy. We have heard, too, that you have determined to go to Wittenberg. Stay for your mother's sake. Stay here, for we love and like to see you, and are unwilling that any harm should happen to you. Stay with us at Court; or, if not, betake yourself to your kingdom.

Queen. My much beloved son, Prince Hamlet, it greatly astonishes me that you have chosen to leave us here, and to betake yourself to Wittenberg. Thou knowest well that your royal father is but lately dead, and that we are grieved at heart to have lost him, and that, if you leave us, our grief will be the greater. Dearest son, then, remain here; and you shall have without restraint whatsoever may please and delight you.

Hamlet. I will obey you with all my heart, and instead of going will stay here.

King. Do so, dearest Prince. But say, Corambus, how is it with your son Leonardus ? Has he already set out for France.

Corambus. Aye, my gracious lord and King, he has gone already.

King. But is this with your consent (*Consens*) ?

Corambus. Aye—Upper Consent, Middle Consent, and Lower Consent. O, Your Highness, he has got an extraordinary, noble, excellent, and glorious Consent (*Consens*) from me.

King. As he has your Consent, so may it go well with me, and may bring him safe back again to us. We have, however, determined to hold a carouse (*Carisell*), whereby our dearest spouse may forget her melancholy. But you, Prince Hamlet, and other nobles like you, must shew yourselves cheerful. For the present, however, we must make an end of our festivities, for the day is coming on to put to flight the black night. Thee, however, my dearest consort, I must follow to your bed-chamber.

Come, let us, hand in hand, and arm and arm embrace ;
Let us enjoy the sweet pledge of love and quiet.

The metre of the original :—

Kommt, lasst uns Hand in Hand, und Arm in Arm
    einschliessen ;
Lasst uns das süsse Pfand der Lieb und Ruh geniessen.

ACT II.

SCENE I.

King, Queen.

King. Dearest consort, how comes it that you are so sad ? You are our Queen. We love you, and all that the kingdom is worth is yours. What is it that troubles you ?

Queen. My King, I am greatly troubled at the melancholy of my son Hamlet. He is my only prince : and this it is that pains me.

King. How! is he melancholy? We will call-in all the excellent doctors and physician of our realm that they may relieve him.

SCENE II.

Corambus (to the preceding).

Corambus. News, my gracious Lord and King.

King. What news?

Corambus. Prince Hamlet is mad; mad as ever the Greek madman.

King. And why is he mad?

Corambus. Because he has lost his wits (*Verstand*).

King. Where has he lost his wits?

Corambus. That's more than I know. He that has found them may perhaps know.

SCENE III.

Ophelia.

Ophelia. Alas! father, protect me.

Corambus. What is it, my child?

Ophelia. Alas! father, it is Prince Hamlet that plagues (*plagt*) me. He lets me have no peace.

Corambus. Make yourself easy, my daughter. He has not done anything else, has he? O! now I know why Prince Hamlet is mad. He is certainly in love with my daughter?

King. Can love then make a man mad?

Corambus. No doubt, my gracious Lord and King, love is full strong enough to make a man mad. I remember myself when I was young how it plagued me—it made me as mad as a March hare (*Märzhaasen*). But I take no note of it. I like better to sit by my fireplace, and count-out my red coins, and drink Your Majesty's health.

King. But cannot one see with one's own eyes his raving and madness ?

Corambus. Yes, your Majesty. We will just move a little aside, and my daughter shall shew him the jewel of which he has made her a present, and then your Majesty can see his madness. [*They hide.*

SCENE ·IV.

Hamlet, Ophelia.

Ophelia. I pray your Highness to take back the jewel with which you presented me.

Hamlet. What, girl! dost thou want a husband. Get thee away from me—no, come back. Hear, girl; you young women do nothing but lead the young men astray. Your beauty you buy of the apothecaries and pedlars. Listen : I will tell you a story. There was once on a time a knight in Anion, who fell in love with a lady, who, to look at, was the Goddess Venus. However, when the bedtime came, the bride went first and began to undress herself. So first she took out an eye which had been fixed in very cunningly ; then her front teeth, made of ivory, so well that the like were not to be seen ; then she washed herself, and away went all the paint she had daubed herself with. And now, when the husband came at last, to embrace her, the moment he saw her he shrank back, for he thought he had seen a spectre. And so it is that such as you take-in the young fellows .So listen to me. But stay, girl! No—go! but not to a nunnery where two pair of slippers be at the bedside.

[*Exit.*

Corambus. Is he not perfectly and veritably mad (*perfect und veritabel toll*), my gracious Lord and King ?

King. Corambus, leave us. When we have need of thee we will send for thee. [*Exit Corambus.*] We have seen this madness and raving of the Prince's with wonder. But it seems to us that this is not genuine madness, but rather an affectation of it. We must contrive that he on his part must be got rid off: or else harm may come of it.

SCENE V.

Hamlet, Horatio.

Hamlet. My excellent friend Horatio, it is through this pretended madness that I hope to get the opportunity of revenging my father's death. You know, however, that my father (*Vater = stepfather*) is always surrounded by guards (*Trabanten*). So it may miscarry. Should you chance to find my dead body, let let it be honorably buried : for at the first occasion that offers itself I will match myself against him.

Horatio. I entreat your Highness to do no such thing. It may be that the Ghost has deceived you.

Hamlet. O no ! his words were too plain. I cannot but believe him. But what news is the fool bringing now ?

SCENE VI.

Corambus, Hamlet.

Corambus. News, my gracious lord ! the actors are come.

Hamlet. When *Marus Russig was an actor in Rome, that was a fine time.

Corambus. Ha ! ha ! ha ! Your Highness is always teasing me.

Hamlet. O ! Jeptha, Jeptha, what a fair daughter thou haddest !

Corambus. Your Highness always will be bringing-in my daughter.

Hamlet. Well, old man ; let the master of company come in.

Corambus. It shall be so.   [*Exit.*

Hamlet. These actors come just in time. I will use them to test the Ghost ; whether he has told the truth or not. I have seen a tragedy acted wherein one brother kills another in a garden ; and this they shall now act. If the king change colour he has done what the Ghost says.

* See pp. 96-7.

SCENE VII.

Actors. Carl, the principal actor.

Carl. May the Gods ever bestow on your Highness blessings, luck, and health.

Hamlet. Thanks, my friend! What can I do for you? '

Carl. With leave, your Highness, we are foreign High German actors. Our wish was to have had the privilege of acting at his Majesty's wedding. But Fortune turned her back, and contrary winds their face, towards us. So we now ask of your Highness leave to represent a story, so that our long journey shall not have been made in vain.

Hamlet. Were you not, some years ago, at the University of Wittenberg. I think I saw you act there.

Carl. Yes, your Highness. We are the same company.

Hamlet. Have you still got the whole company?

Carl. We are not so strong; since some students took appointments in Hamburg. Still we are enough for many pleasant Comedies and Tragedies.

Hamlet. Can you give us a play this very night?

Carl. Yes, your Highness, we are strong enough and in practice enough for that.

Hamlet. Have you still the three actresses with you? They used to act well.

Carl. No, only two. One stayed behind with her husband at the Court of Saxony.

Hamlet. When you were at Wittenberg you acted good Comedies: only you had some fellows among you who had good clothes but dirty shirts, and some who had boots but no spurs.

Carl. Your Highness, it is generally a hard matter to get everything. Perhaps, they thought they would not have to ride.

Hamlet. Still it is better to have everything correct (*accurat*): so listen a little longer, and excuse me : for it is not often that you can hear at first hand what the lookers-on think of you. There were others among you who had silk

K

stockings and white shoes, but with black hats on their
heads: and with about as many feathers below as above. I
think they must have gone to bed with them as nightcaps.
That's bad, and is easily altered. You may, too, as well tell
some of them that when they act the part of a king or a
prince they should not leer when they pay compliments to
ladies, and not be such peacock-strutting Hidalgos (*Spa-
nischer Pfauentritte*) and put on such bravado airs (*Fechter-
mienen*). A man of rank laughs at such things. Natural
ease is the best. He who plays a king must fancy that, during the play he is a king; and a peasant must be a peasant.

Carl. I take your Highness' correction with humble
respect, and we will try to do better for the future.

Hamlet. I am a great lover of your art and only speak to
you for the best; for it is a mirror in which one may see
one's own failings. Listen. You acted at Wittenberg a
piece about King *Pir-*, *Pir-*,—it *pir*red so.

Carl. Ah! it was perhaps one about the great King
Pyrrhus.[1]

Hamlet. Methinks it was; but I am not quite sure.

Carl. Would your Highness name a character in it, or
say what it was about?

Hamlet. It was about one brother murdering another in a
garden.

Carl. That's the piece. Did not the King's brother pour
oil into the King's ear?

Hamlet. He did. That's it. Can you play that piece
this evening?

Carl. O, Yes! Easily enough, for there are not many
characters.

Hamlet. Well, then, get the stage ready in the great hall.
If you want any timber get them of the architect; if anything from the armoury, or anything in the way of clothes,
ask the Master of the Robes or the Steward. We wish you
to have whatever is wanted.

Carl. We humbly thank your Highness for these favours;
and will set about it at once. Farewell.   [*Exit.*

---

[1] *Vide* Note 1, p. 144.

Hamlet. These actors come most opportunely. Horatio, keep an eye on the king and see whether he turn pale or change colour : for if he do he has done the deed. These players with their feigned stories often put on the truth. I'll tell you a pretty tale. There was a pretty case in Germany near Strasburg. A wife had murdered her husband by piercing him through the heart with a shoemaker's awl; and then, with the help of her paramour, buried him under the doorstep. So matters stood for as long as nine years : when certain actors came that way and acted a tragedy containing a similar incident. The wife, who was sitting with her paramour at the play, was touched in her conscience, and, began to cry aloud and to shriek " Woe is me ! that touches me ! So it was that I killed my husband." She tore her hair, ran out of the theatre to the judge, confest, of her own accord, the murder, and as this was found to be true, she in deep repentance for her crime, received the consolations of a priest, and, in true contrition gave up her body to the executioner, and commended her soul to Heaven. Oh that my uncle and father would thus take his crime upon himself, if he be guilty. Come, Horatio, we will go and await the King. Pray, however, take note of everything, for I must feign.

Horatio. Your Highness I will bid my eyes look out sharply. *[Exeunt.*

SCENE VIII.

King, Queen, Hamlet, Horatio, Corambus, Courtiers.

King. My dearest consort, I hope that now you will banish your melancholy, and let it give place to joy; for there is to be, before supper, a comedy by some German actors, and after supper, a ballet (*ballet*) by our own people.

Queen. I shall be glad to witness such mirth : but I doubt whether my heart will be at ease, for I know not how it is, but some approaching mischief disturbs my spirit.

King. Be easy. Prince Hamlet, we understand that some

actors have arrived and that they will act a comedy this evening. Tell us : Is it so ?

Hamlet. Aye, my father, it is. They have asked a favour and I have given them permission. I hope it is approved by Your Majesty.

King. What is the plot ? There is nothing in it offensive or rude ?

Hamlet. It is a good plot. We who have good consciences are not touched by it.

King. What are they waiting for ? Let them begin. We would see what these Germans can do.

Hamlet. Marshall, see that they get ready : tell them to begin.

Corambus. Holla you Comedians ! Where are you ! You are to begin at once. Ah ! here they come.

> [*Dumb Show. The King with his Queen. He will lie down to sleep. The Queen prevents him. He lies down nevertheless. The Queen kisses him and takes her leave. The King's brother comes with a phial and pours something into his ear.*

Hamlet. That is King Pyrrhus who goes to sleep in the garden. The Queen begs him not to do so ; however he lies down. The poor wife goes away. Then, see, the King's brother comes with the juice of eben and pours it into the King's ear, which, as soon as ever it mixes with the blood of man, destroys the body.

King. Torches ! lanterns ! the play displeases us.

Corambus. Pages, lackies (*pagen, lackeyen*), light the torches. The King is going away. Quick. Light-up. The players have made a mess of it.

> [*Exeunt King, Queen, Corambus, Courtiers.*

Hamlet. "Torches, the play displeases us." Seest thou not that Ghost has not deceived us ? Actors ! go and take this from me, that though the matter be not brought to an end and the King be displeased, I am well satisfied, and, in my behalf, Horatio shall satisfy you.

Carl. We thank you ; and, further ask the favour of a pass-port.

Hamlet. You shall have one. [*Exeunt actors*]. Now can I go on boldly with my revenge. Sawest thou how the King changed colour when he saw the play?

Horatio. I did, your Highness; that's certain.

Hamlet. Even so: my father was done to death just as it was in the play. But I will pay the murderer off for the evil deed.

SCENE IX.

Enter Corambus.

Corambus. The actors will get but a sorry recompense, for their action has sorely displeased the King.

Hamlet. What sayest thou, old man; will they get a sorry recompense? The worse they are rewarded by the King the better they will be rewarded by Heaven.

Corambus. Can, your Highness! actors really get into Heaven?

Hamlet. What, you old fool, do you fancy that they won't find room there? Be off, and treat them well.

Corambus. Aye, aye. I'll treat them as they deserve.

Hamlet. Treat them, I say, well: for there is no greater credit to be got than through actors, since they travel both far and wide. If they be treated well in one play, they cannot crack too much of it in another; for their Theatrum is a little world wherein they represent nearly all that takes place in the great world. They revive the old forgotten histories, and set before us good examples; they publish abroad the justice and praiseworthy government of princes; they punish vice and exalt virtue; they praise the good; and show how tyranny is punished. Therefore should you treat them well.

Corambus. Well, they shall have their reward as they are such great people. Farewell, Your Highness. [*Exit.*

Hamlet. Come, Horatio, I am going; aud from this hour, all my thoughts are bent on finding the King alone, that I may take his life as he has taken my father's.

Horatio. Pray, Your Highness, be prudent, lest you yourself come to harm.

Hamlet. I shall, I must, I will revenge myself on the murderer ;

If I cannot do it by stratagem, I will break-out in violence.

The metre of the original.

Ich soll, ich muss, ich will mich an den Mörder rächen,

Kann ich mit List nichts thun, will ich mit Macht durchbrechen.

ACT III.

SCENE I.

Here is presented an Altar in a Temple.
(Hier präsentirt sich im Tempel ein Altar.)

King (alone). Now begins my conscience to awaken ; the remorse for my treachery to prick me sharply. It is time that I turn to repentance, and confess to Heaven my perpetrated crime. I fear my guilt is so great that they never can forgive me. Nevertheless I will pray to the Gods from the bottom of my heart that they will forgive my grievous sins.   [*Kneels before the altar.*

SCENE II.

Hamlet, with a naked sword.

Thus long have I followed the damned dog, and now I have found him. Now is the time, when he is alone. I will take his life while——[*Is about to stab him.*] But no. I will first let him finish his prayer. But now, when I think of it, he did not give my father time for a prayer, but sent him to Hell sleeping and, perhaps, in his sins. Therefore will I send him to the same place [*will again run him through from behind*]. But hold, Hamlet ! Why shouldest thou take his sins upon thee? I will let him end his prayer, and escape this time, and · give him his life: but at some other time I will have my full revenge. [*Exit.*

King. My conscience is somewhat lightened; but still the dog lies gnawing at my heart. Now will I go hence, and with fastings, and alms, and fervent prayers, reconcile the Highest. Cursed ambition, to what hast thou brought me! [*Exit.*

SCENE III.

Queen, Corambus.

Queen. Corambus, say how is it with my son, Prince Hamlet. Does his madness abate at all, or will his raving never end.

Corambus. Ah, no, Your Majesty, he is just as mad as ever.

SCENE IV.

Horatio.

Horatio. Most gracious Queen, Prince Hamlet is in the antechamber, and craves a private audience (*Audienz*).

Queen. He is very dear to us; so let him come in at once.

Horatio. It shall be done, Your Majesty. [*Exit.*

Queen. Corambus, hide yourself behind the tapestry, till we call you. '

Corambus. Ay, ay, your Majesty, I will. [*Hides himself.*

SCENE V.

Hamlet, Queen.

Hamlet. Mother! did you know your late husband well?

Queen. Ah! remind me not of my former grief. I cannot but weep when I think of it.

Hamlet. Weep! Leave-off weeping. They are but crocodile's tears. But see. Yonder in that gallery hangs the counterfeit (*Conterfait*) of your first husband, and there hangs the counterfeit of your present. What thinkest thou? Which is the comelier of the two? Is not the first a majestic nobleman (*majestätischer Herr*)?

Queen. He is indeed. That is true.

Hamlet. And yet thou hast so soon forgotten him. Fie, for shame! You have had almost on the same day the burial and the betrothal. But, hush, are all the doors closed?

Queen. Why do you ask?

                 [*Corambus coughs behind the tapestry.*

Hamlet. Who is that who is listening to us? [*Stabs him.*

Corambus. Woe is me, O Prince. What hast thou done? I am dying.

Queen. O Heavens, my son, what are you doing? It is Corambus, the Chamberlain.

SCENE VI.

Ghost passes across the stage. [*Thunder and lightning.*]

Hamlet. Ah, noble spirit of my father, stay. What would'st thou? Criest thou for vengeance? Thou shalt have it at the right time.

Queen. What are you about? Who are you talking to?

Hamlet. Seest thou not the spirit of thy departed husband? See, he beckons as if he would speak to you.

Queen. How? I see nothing.

Hamlet. I believe you. You *do* see nothing; for you are no longer worthy to look on his form. Fie, for shame! Not one word more will I say to you.   [*Exit.*

Queen (alone). O God! how has this melancholy brought upon the Prince this raving? Alas, my own son has wholly lost his senses. And, alas! alas! I am much to blame. Had I not wedded my brother-in-law, my first husband's brother, I had not robbed my son of the Crown of Denmark. But when a thing is done what can we? Nothing. Matters must stand as they are. If the Pope had not allowed the marriage it would never have taken place. I will go hence, and do my best to restore my son to his former sense and health.

SCENE VII.

Jens, alone.

Jens. It is long since I went to Court to pay my taxes. I am afraid that, go where I may, I shall be put into jail. I wish I could only find some good friend who would speak a good word for me, so that I might get-off.

SCENE VIII.

Phantasmo.

Phantasmo. There are strange goings-on at Court. Prince Hamlet is mad, and Ophelia is mad too. In short (*in Summa*) things go on so very queerly that I have half a mind to run away.

Jens. By all that's holy, there is my good old friend Phantasmo. No better man could I hit upon. I will ask him to say a good word for me. Holla! Master Phantasmo !

Phantasmo. Thanks ! What can I do for you, Mister Bumpkin ?

Jens. Ah, my good Master Phantasmo. 'Tis a long time since I was at Court, and I am a long way behind-hand. Put in a good word for me and I will reward you with a good cheese.

Phantasmo. What ! Dost thou think, Master Clown, that at Court I get nothing to eat ?

SCENE IX.

Ophelia mad.

Ophelia. I run and run and cannot find my sweetheart. He has sent to me to come to him. We are to be married ;

and I am dressed for it already. But there he is, my Love !
Oh, my lambkin, I have sought you everywhere ; everywhere have I sought you. But think, the tailor has spoilt
my cotton (*cattuner*) gown. See, there is a pretty flower
for you, my Heart !

Phantasmo. Oh, the Devil ! I wish she were away. She
fancies I am her sweetheart.

Ophelia. What sayest thou, my Love ! We will go to
bed together. I will wash you quite clean.

Phantasmo. Aye, aye ; I'll soap you, and wash you out
too.

Ophelia. Hark, my Love, hast thou already put on your
fine new suit ? Aye. That is well made ; quite according
to the new fashion (*die neue Mode*).

Phantasmo. I know that without—

Ophelia. Oh, Lord, I had nearly forgotten. The King
has invited me to supper and I must make haste. My
coach ! my coach !   [*Exit.*

Phantasmo. O Hecate, thou Queen of witches, how glad
I am that mad thing is off. If she had stayed any longer
I should have been mad myself. I must get away before
the foolish woman comes again.

Jens. O kind Master Phantasmo ! Pray do not forget
me.

Phantasmo. Come along, Bumpkin. We'll see what
we can do.   [*Exeunt.*

SCENE X.

King, Hamlet, Horatio, Two Attendants.

King. Where is the body of Corambus ! Has it not yet
been removed ?

Horatio. It is still lying in the place where it was stuck
through.

King. It grieves us that he has lost his life so suddenly.
Go, let it be taken away. We wish it to be honorably
buried. Oh, Prince Hamlet, what hast thou done to stab

an old and harmless man! It grieves us to our heart; but
as it has been done unwittingly, this murder is in some
degree excusable. I fear, however, that when it gets
known among the nobility they will raise a rebellion among
my subjects; and, then, they may revenge his death on
you. However, in our fatherlike care for you, we have
devised a plan to ward off this danger from you.

Hamlet. I am sorry for it, my Lord Uncle and Father.
I had wished to say something in private to the Queen,
when he lay in wait for me as a spy. I did not, however,
know that it was this fool. But how would your Majesty
have us proceed (*procediren*)?

King. We have resolved to send you to England because
the English Crown is friendly to our own. You can there
refresh yourself for a while, since the air there is better
than ours and may promote your recovery. We will give
you some of our own attendants, who shall accompany you
and serve you faithfully.

Hamlet. Ay, ay, King, send me off to * Portugal so that
I may never come back again. That's the better plan.

King. No, not to Portugal, but to England, and those
two shall accompany you on the journey. But when you
arrive in England you shall have more attendants.

Hamlet. Those are the lackeys (*Laquaien*), are they?
Nice fellows!

King [apart to the two attendants]. Listen, you two. As
soon as you have reached England do as I have ordered
you. Get a sword or a pistol each and take his life. But
should this attempt miscarry, take this letter and present
it along with the Prince to the place for which it is addressed. There he will be so well looked to that he will
never come back from England again. But in this point be
cautious. Reveal your business to no man. You shall receive your reward as soon as ever you return.

Hamlet. Well, your Majesty, who are they, then, that are
to bear me company?

* See pp. 100--103.

King. These two. The Gods be with you; and give you a fair wind for the place and spot you are going to.

Hamlet. Now Adieu, my Lady Mother. (*Nun Adieu, Frau Mutter.*)

King. How is this, Prince? why do you call me Mother?

Hamlet. Man and wife are one flesh. Father or Mother —it is all the same to me.

King. Well! Fare thee well. Heaven bless you.

[*Exit.*

Hamlet. Now, you noble sneaks (*Quantschen*), are you to be my companions?

Both. We are, my Lord.

Hamlet. Come, then, my noble (*noblen*) comrades, let us be off, off for England.

[*Exeunt.*

SCENE XI.

Phantasmo, Ophelia.

Phantasmo. Going or standing, that high-flying maiden, that Ophelia is after me at every corner. I can get no peace. She says I am her lover; and I am not, If I could but hide myself somewhere where she could not find.

Ophelia. Where is my sweetheart. The rogue will not stay with me. Ever away—but, see, there he is. Listen, my Love, I have been with the priest, and he will join (*copuliren*) us this very day. I have made all ready for the wedding—chicken, hares, meat, butter, and cheese—all bought. There is nothing now wanting but the musicians (*Musikanten*) to play us to bed.

Phantasmo. I can only say, Yes. Come, then, let's go to bed together.

Ophelia. No, no, my puppet, we must first go with one another to Church, and then we'll eat and drink and dance; that we will. We will be right merry!

Phantasmo. Aye, aye, right merry; three eating out of one dish.

Ophelia. What do you say? If you won't have me, I'll not have you [*strikes him*]. Look yonder! That's my Love there. He is making signs to me. See what a fine suit of clothes he has. See, he is enticing me to him. He will throw me a lily and a rose. He will take me in his arms. He is making signs to me. I am coming; I am coming.

[*Exit.*

Phantasmo. At close quarters she's barely sensible, and at a fair distance she's downright mad. I wish she were hanged, and then the carrion could not run after me so.

[*Exit.*

ACT IV.

Hamlet, Two Ruffians (Banditen).

Hamlet. There's a pleasant place here on this island. We'll bide here awhile, and dine. There's a pleasant wood, and cool stream of water. So bring me of the best from the ship; for here we'll enjoy ourselves.

First Ruffian. My Lord and Grace, this is no time for eating; for from this island you will never depart. Here is the spot which is chosen for your churchyard.

Hamlet. What sayest thou, base slave? Knowest thou whom I am? Would you pass jests on a Prince Royal? However, for this time, I forgive you.

Second Ruffian. It is no jest. It is downright earnest.

Hamlet. Why this? What injury have I ever done you? For my part I can think of none. Why, then, such bad thoughts?

First Ruffian. It is our orders, from the King, as soon we get Your Highness on this island, we are to take your life.

Hamlet. My dear friends, spare my life. Say that you have done your work; and so long as I live I will never come in sight of the King. Think well whether you do yourselves good by having on your hands the blood of an innocent Prince ? Will you stain your consciences with my sins ? Alas, that in an evil hour like this I have no weapon ? If I had but something in my hands—

[*Makes an attempt to seize a sword.*

Second Ruffian. Holla, Comrade ? Look out for your weapon.

First Ruffian. I'll look-out. Now, Prince, prepare yourself. We have no time to lose.

Hamlet. Since it cannot be otherwise, and I must die at your hands at the bidding of a tyrannical King, I must submit, although innocent. And you, driven to the deed by poverty, I willingly forgive. My blood, however, must be answered for by the fratricide and parricide at the great day of Judgement.

First Ruffian. What have we to do with the great day ? To-day is the day for our business.

Second Ruffian. True brother! Let us set to. Let us fire ; you from one side and I on the other.

Hamlet. Hear me but for one word. Even the very worst of criminals would not be denied a time to repent in. I pray you, then, an innocent Prince as I am, to let me address to my Maker an earnest prayer; after this I am ready to die. But I will make a sign. I will turn my hands towards Heaven, and the moment I stretch out my arms you can fire. One of you aim on one side, and the other on the other; and when I say " Fire " give me what I need. Be sure to hit me so that I shall not be long in torment.

Second Ruffian. Well, we may do as much as this for you ; so go on.

Hamlet [*separates his hands from one another*]. Fire. [*Throws himself forward between the two, who shoot one another*]. O just Heaven, I thank you for this heavenly idea, and I will always reverence the guardian angel who through this happy thought has saved my life. For these rascals, however, the recompense has been suitable to the deed. But the dog still moves; they have shot one another. However, I give the last stroke to my revenge, and make sure: else one of the rogues may escape [*stabs one of them with his own sword*]. Now will I see whether they have any secret with them. This one has nothing. On the murderer, however, I find a letter; which I will make free to read. This letter is written to the arch-murderer in England, that, in case this attempt fail, they should just make me over to him, and he would just blow out the light of my life. However, the Gods stand by the upright man. Now will I return to the terror of my father. But I will not trust any longer to water, for who knows but what the ship's captain is a villain. I will go to the first station and take post. The sailors I will order (*commandiren*) back to Denmark. This rascal, however, I will throw into the water.

[*Exit.*

SCENE II.

King, with Attendants.

King. We wish to find out how it goes with our son, Prince Hamlet, and whether the men whom we sent with him fellow-travellers have dealt honorably with him, even as we commanded.

SCENE III.

Phantasmo, King.

Phantasmo. News, Mister (*Monsieur*) King! Brand-new news!

King. What is it, Phantasmo?

Phantasmo. Leonhardus has come home from France.

King. That pleases us. Let him present himself.

SCENE IV.

Leonhardus, King.

Leonhardus. My gracious Lord and King, I demand of

your Majesty either my father or revenge for his lamentable murder. If this be not forthcoming I shall forget that you are King, and myself take my own vengeance on the murderer.

King. Leonhardus, be satisfied that we are guiltless of your father's death. Prince Hamlet has unaware run him through behind the hangings, but we will see that he is punished for it.

Leonardus. As your Majesty is guiltless of my father's death, I fall on my knees and beg for pardon. My anger as well as my filial affection had so overcome me that I knew not what I did.

King. You are forgiven. We can easily believe that it touches you nearly to have lost your father so miserably. But rest satisfied—you shall find a father in ourselves.

Leonardus. I thank you for this great act of royal kindness.

SCENE V.

Phantasmo.

Phantasmo. Uncle, King, more news still!

King. What is your new news?

Phantasmo. Prince Hamlet has come back.

King. The Devil you mean, not Prince Hamlet.

Phantasmo. I mean Prince Hamlet, not the Devil.

King. Leonhardus, hear! Now you can avenge your father's death, since the Prince has returned: but you must promise on your oath not to reveal it to any one.

Phantasmo. Doubt me not, your Majesty. Whatsoever your Majesty may reveal shall be kept as silent as if it had been spoken to a stone.

King. We will get-up a fencing-match between you and him. You shall fence with foils. The one who make the first three hits wins a Neapolitan horse. In the middle, however, of the fencing you shall let your foil drop, and take-up instead of it an unblunted weapon, which shall be made exactly like the foil, and be ready to your hand.

This you anoint with a strong poison : and as soon as you shall have wounded him he will die. So will you win both the prize and the king's favour.

Leonhardus. Your Majesty must excuse me. The Prince is so good a fencer that he might turn my own weapon against me.

King. Leonhardus, don't hesitate to do it ; whether it be to please your King or to revenge your father. As your father's murderer the Prince deserves such a death. We, however, cannot enforce the law against him, for he has his lady mother to back him, and my subjects love him much. Hence, if we openly avenged ourselves, there might easily be a rebellion. To shun him both as stepson and kinsman is only an act of righteous justice ; for he is murderous and he is beside himself, and we must for the future, even on our account, be afraid of such a wicked man. Do then what we desire, and you will relieve your King of his fears, and yourself take, without being discovered, a revenge for your father's murder.

Leonhardus. It is a hard matter and one which I scarcely like : for should the matter get abroad it would certainly cost me my life.

King. Do not hesitate. Should this fail we have thought of another trick. We will have an eastern diamond powdered fine, and when he is heated present it to him in a beaker mixed with wine and sugar. So shall he drink his death to our healths.

Leonhardus. Well then, Your Majesty, under this safeguard, I'll do the deed.

SCENE VI.

Queen.

Queen. Gracious Lord and King, dearest husband, I bring you bad news.

King. What is it, my dearest soul ?

Queen. My favorite maid-of-honour, Ophelia, runs up and

L

down, and cries, and screams, and eats nothing, and drinks nothing. They say she has quite lost her wits.

King. Alas! one hears nothing but thoroughly sad and unhappy tidings.

SCENE VII.

Ophelia, with flowers.

Ophelia. See! there! you have a flower; and you; and you. [*Gives each a flower.*] But what, odds bodikins! what had I all but forgotten? I must run quick. I have forgotten my ornaments. Ah, my diadem.(*Front*). I must go at once to the Court Jeweller, and ask what new fashions (*neue Moden*) he has got. So, so; lay out the table quickly. I shall soon be back.   [*Runs off.*

Leonhardus. Am I, then, born to miseries of all sorts! My father is dead; my sister is robbed of her wits. My heart well nigh bursts for grief.

King. Leonhardus, be satisfied: you shall live alone in our favour. But do you, dearest Queen, be pleased to walk within with us, for we have something secret to reveal to you. Leonhardus do not forget what we have said to you.

Queen. My King, we must think of something by which this unfortunate maiden may be restored to her senses.

King. Let the case be laid before our own physician. But do you, Leonhardus, follow us.

———

ACT V.

SCENE I.

Hamlet.

Hamlet. Unfortunate Prince! how much longer shalt thou remain restless? How long will you, O righteous Nemesis, before you have sharpened your just sword of vengeance for my fratricide uncle? Hither have I come again, yet I cannot obtain my revenge. The fratricide is surrounded by so many retainers. But I swear that, before the sun has made his journey from east to west, I will revenge myself on him.

SCENE II.

Horatio.

Horatio. It rejoices me to see your Highness back and in good health. Prythee, however, tell me why you have returned so soon.

Hamlet. Ah, Horatio, you have nearly missed never seeing me again alive; for my life has been at stake; only the Almighty power has specially protected me.

Horatio. What says Your Highness? How was it?

Hamlet. Thou knowest that the King had given me a couple of fellow-travellers as attendants and companions. Now it so happened that, for two days, we had contrary (*contrairen*) winds. So we had to anchor on an island near Dover. I went with my two companions from the ship to get a little fresh air. Then came the cursed rascals and would have had my life, and said that the King had bribed them to it. I begged hard for my life, and promised them a handsome reward, and that, if they reported me to the King as dead, I would never go near the court again. But there was no compassion in them. At last, the Gods put something into my head: and I begged them that, before my death, I might make a prayer, and that when I cried "Fire" they would fire. But, even as I gave the word, I fell on the ground, and they shot one another. It is thus that I have this time escaped with my life. My arrival, however, will be no good news to the King.

Horatio. Oh! unheard-of treachery!

SCENE III.

Phantasmo.

Hamlet. Look, Horatio, the fool is far dearer to the King than I.

Phantasmo. Welcome home, Prince Hamlet! Knowest thou the news? The King has laid a wager on you and the young Leonhardus. You are to fight with foils; and he who makes the first two hits is to win a white Neapolitan horse.

Hamlet. It is certain that this is the case?

Phantasmo. It is certainly no other than as I say.

Hamlet. Horatio, what can this mean? I and Leonhardus to fight one another? I fancy they have told this fool something wonderful, for one can make him believe what one will. Look now, Signora (*sic*) Phantasmo, it is terribly cold.

Phantasmo. Aye, it is terribly cold.

[*Shivers, with chattering teeth.*

Hamlet. And now it is not so cold.

Phantasmo. Aye aye, it is just the happy medium.

Hamlet. But now it is very hot. [*Wipes his face.*

Phantasmo. Oh, what a terribly heat!

[*Wipes away the perspiration.**

Hamlet. And now it is neither hot nor cold.

Phantasmo. Yes! it is now just temperate (*recht temperirt*).

Hamlet. You see, Horatio, one can just make him believe what one will. Phantasmo, go to the King and say that I will soon wait on him. [*Exit Phantasmo.*

Hamlet. Come now, Horatio, I will go at once and present myself to the King. But what? What means this? My nose bleeds, and my whole body is ashake. [*Swoons.*

Horatio. Most serene Prince. Heavens! what means this? Be yourself again, my Lord. What ails you, my Lord?

Hamlet. I know not, Horatio. When the thought struck me of returning to the Court, a sudden faintness came over me. What this means the Gods only know.

Horatio. Ah, Heaven grant that this omen (*omen*) be no unlucky one.

Hamlet. Be it what it may, I'll to the Court, even though it cost me my life. [*Exit.*

* See pp. 98-9.

SCENE IV.

King, Leonhardus, Phantasmo.

King. Leonhardus, get ready, for Prince Hamlet will soon be here.

Leonhardus. I am, Your Majesty, already prepared, and I will, at least, do my best.

King. Look well to it! Here comes the Prince——

SCENE V.

Hamlet. Horatio.

Hamlet. All health and happiness to your Majesty!

King. We thank you, Prince! We are greatly rejoiced that the melancholy has in some degree left you. Wherefore we have appointed a friendly contest between yourself and the young Leonhardus. You are to fight with foils, and the one who makes the first three hits shall have won a white Neapolitan horse, with saddle-cloths and trappings to match.

Hamlet. Your Majesty must pardon me; for I have had but little practice in foil; Leonhardus, however, has just come from France, so that he is doubtless in good practice. I pray, then, that for this reason you may excuse me.

King. Do it, Prince Hamlet, to gratify us; for we are desirous of knowing what sort of feints there are in Germany and France.

SCENE VI.

Queen.

Queen. My gracious Lord and King, I have a sad calamity to tell you.

King. Heaven forbid! What is it?

Queen. Ophelia has gone to the top of a high hill, and has thrown herself down, and has killed [2] herself.

Leonhardus. Unfortunate Leonhardus! Thou hast lost within a short space of time both a father and a sister

[2] See Note, p. 145.

Whither will misfortune lead you! I could myself die of weariness.

King. Be comforted, Leonardus. We are gracious to you. Only begin the contest. Phantasmo, bring the foils. Horatio, you shall be umpire.

Phantasmo. Here is the warm beer.

Hamlet. Come on, Leonhardus; and let us to see which of us is to fit the other with the fool's cap (*wer dem andern die Schellen wird anhängen*). Should I, however, go wrong (*einer exces begehen*) pray excuse (*excusiren*) me, for it is long since I have tried the foils.

Leonhardus. I am your Highness' servant: but you are only jesting.

[*The first bout they fight fair. Leonhardus is hit.*

Hamlet. That's one, Leonhardus!

Leonhardus. True, your Highness. Now for my revenge (*Revange*). [*He drops his foil, and takes up the poisoned sword which lies ready to his hand (parat), and gives the Prince a thrust in carte in the arm. Hamlet parries on Leonhardus, so that they both drop their weapons; and each runs to pick one up. Hamlet gets the poisoned, one and wounds Leonhardus mortally.*]

Leonhardus. Woe is me! I have had a mortal thrust. I have been paid in my own coin. Heaven have mercy on me!

Hamlet. What the Devil is this, Leonhardus? Have I wounded you with the foil? How can this be?

King. Go quick, and get my royal goblet with some wine, so that the combatants may recruit themselves a little. Go, Phantasmo, and fetch it. [*Descends from the throne. Aside.*] I hope that when they both drink of the wine they may both die; and, then, no one will know of the plot.

Hamlet. Tell me, Leonhardus! how did all this come about?

Leonardus. Alas, Prince, I have been seduced into this misfortune by the King! See what it is that you have in your hand! It is a poisoned sword.

Hamlet. O heaven ! what is this ?   Save me from it.

Leonhardus. I was to have wounded you with it, for it is
so strongly poisoned that the man who takes from it even
a scratch, must forthwith die.

King. Ho, gentlemen ! pause for a minute and drink.
[*While the King is rising from his chair and speaking these
words, the Queen takes the cup out of Phantasmo's hand, and
drinks.   The King cries out.*]   Ho ! where is the goblet ?
Alas, best of wives, what art thou doing ?   Its contents are
deadly poison ?   Alas, alas, what hast thou done ?

Queen. Alas, I am dying !

Hamlet. And thou, tyrant, shall accompany her in her
death.   [*Stabs him from behind.*

King. Woe is me !   I am receiving my bad recompense.

Leonhardus. Adieu (*sic*) Prince Hamlet !   Adieu, world !
I am dying also.   Prince, pardon me !

Hamlet. May Heaven receive thy soul; for thou art guiltless.   But as to this tyrant—let him wash himself of his
black sins in Hell.   Ah ! Horatio, now is my spirit at rest,
for now have I revenged myself on my enemies.   I, too,
have taken a hit on my arm; but I hope it is no importance.
I grieve that I have hit Leonhardus; though I don't know
how I got the sword into my hand.   But as is the work so
are the wages.   He has received his reward.   Nothing
afflicts me more than my Lady mother.   Still, she has de-
served this death for her sins.   But tell me, who gave her
the cup that has poisoned her ?

Phantasmo. I, Prince.   I also brought the poisoned sword;
but the poisoned wine was to be drunk by no one but yourself.

Hamlet. Hast thou also been an instrument in all this
misery ?   There !   That is your reward.

                                      [*Stabs him mortally.*

Phantasmo. Stab away ; and may the blade hurt you.

Hamlet. Alas, Horatio, I fear that with all my revenge it
will cost me my life ; for I am badly wounded in the arm.
I am getting faint, my limbs become weak, my legs will not

bear me; my voice fails; I feel the poison in all my limbs. I pray you, dear Horatio, to carry my crown to Norway, to my cousin, the Duke Fortempras (*sic*) so that the kingdom may not fall into other hands. Alas! I am dying.

Horatio. Alas, most noble Prince, thou may still look for aid! O Heaven, he is going-off in my arms! What has this kingdom, for a length of time, not undergone from hard wars? Scarcely is there Peace, but internal disturbance, ambition, faction, and murder fill the land. In no age of the world could this lamentable tragedy have been enacted as it has now, alas! been played at this Court. I will, with the help of the faithful councillors, make all preparations that these three high personages (*personen*) shall be interred according to their rank. Then will I at once (*cito*) make for Norway with the crown, and deliver it as this unfortunate Prince has commanded.

> So is it when a Prince forces himself to the crown with
> cunning;
> And by treachery obtains the same;
> He himself experiences nothing but mere mockery and
> scorn;
> For even as the labour so is the reward.

> So gehts wenn ein Regent mit List zur Kron sich dringet,
> Und durch Verrätherey diesselbe an sich bringet,
> Derselb' erlebet nichts, als lauter Spott und Hohn,
> Denn wie die Arbeit ist, so folget auch der Lohn.

Note 1.

This Pyrrhus is the king of Epirus. Here he is the murdered man. In Shakespear he is the son of Achilles, and the hero of the passage by which Hamlet tries the Player. But he is not this purely and simply. In Shakespear he is mainly the Neoptole-mus of the second Æneid of Virgil. But he is this, not so much as a Pyrrhus of Shakspear's own making as the Pyrrhus of play on the subject of Dido, Queen of Carthage. Of this play we believe that we have the full text in Marlowe's drama so named. Here, however, we find the following lines:

> At which the frantic queen leap'd on his face;
> And in his eyelids hanging by the nails
> A little while prolonged her husband's life.
>
> ACT ii., SCENE i.

It is submitted that the Pyrrhus here is the Pyr-rhus of the Hecuba of Euripides, and that, moreover, he is confounded with Polymnestor. If so, there is the probability in favour of the " Hecuba " having been acted in England before the time of Marlowe; and, if this be the case, we see our way towards the origin of the Ghost: for the Ghost of Hamlet's father is, *mutatis mutandis*, the Ghost of Polydorus.

———

NOTE 2.

As there is no burial of Ophelia there is no scene in the churchyard, no Gravediggers, no Yoric. Name for name the " *Yorick* " of Shakespear seems to be the " *Eric* " of the present play. If so, the King is his own Jester. Be it so. A *Chronicon Erici Regis* actually exists. A *Gesta Erici Regis* may have existed. Hence, by a confusion of which we only get a general notion, out of " *Gesta Erici Regis* " may have come " *Yorick the King's Jester.*" In Argen-tile and Curan *Eric*, as here, is the name of the wicked uncle. This manifestly points to some source

M

or sources for the story of Hamlet beyond the four corners of Saxo's narrative.

Ophelia's madness consists chiefly in the mistake of one man for another. In the " Two Noble Kinsmen " it is closely interwoven with the plot. In Shakespear we only find it in the snatch beginning:

" And how should I your truelove know," &c.

This is in favour of the madness of both the Ophelia of Shakespear and the Jailer's Daughter of Fletcher having been drawn from a common source— possibly the present play. This, however, we can scarcely assume without knowing more than we do of the old play of " Palamon and Arcite."

*   *   *   *   *

Such is the likeness and such the difference. The amount of each is left to decision of the reader. It is not too much to say, and it is hoped that it may be said, without discourtesy, that, in nine cases out of ten, the decision will not be wholly unbiassed. Possibly, in the case of any dramatist but Shakespear, the allusion to Portugal would be allowed to settle the question. Less than this has, certainly, settled many similar ones. But, even about the construction of the plot, theories without number have been invented: theories that many influential commentators can scarcely be expected to abandon. Still, as much as possible, the two texts are left to speak for themselves ; at the same time there are a few points upon which the present writer would scarcely do justice to his doctrine if he left them unnoticed.

In the first place the dramatic exposition of an action or a situation is one thing : the mere state-

ment that such an action or situation occurred,
another. It is one thing to describe in a good
business-like prosaic manner the way in which the
elder Hamlet was poisoned; it is another thing to
describe the poisoning as Shakespear does. The
same applies to the situation of Hamlet with his
drawn sword, and the wicked uncle at prayer. The
idea of sparing the murderer until he is certain of
eternal condemnation, though sufficiently devilish, is
poetic or prosaic according to the mode of exhibit-
ing it.

Secondly, we must not only note what we find
in the German play, but what we miss. Thus—

a. Of instances of realistic imagery such as, "not
a mouse stirring," we find none.

b. Of ironical bits of cynicism, such as,

"We would obey her were she ten times our mother,"
not one.

c. Of the soliloquies not one.

Of hypotheses by which the difference may be
accounted for, I know but one; and to the notice of
this I limit myself. It is, as has been already stated,
that the German play is the play of Shakespear
corrupted, attenuated, shorn of its great nobility,
distorted, degraded, vulgarized. But was the German
stage thus much below the English? or even if it
were so, how do we reconcile the recognition of the
poetical element (such as it is) as shown by the Prologue, with the eschewal of it as manifested by the
elimination of the soliloquies?

Again, it is not denied that, what with the
existence of imperfect texts, and what with "stuff"
sometimes "foisted in," and sometimes omitted, by

the players much may be achieved. But time is an element in such a process as this : and here we have something like tangible *data* to go by ; or, at any rate, there are certain limits within which we must confine the effects of what we may call the wear-and-tear of time, and, there are also, criteria by which we may measure the inferiority (real or imaginary) of the German stage to the English. In neither case have we much latitude.

" Hamlet," by no means, stands alone.

The note in page 106 gives us the date of the MS. from which the text is taken. That of the first · representation of the play is, of course, a wholly different matter. Neither, however, can be got at absolutely. Nevertheless, the piece was acted twice, at least, before 1778; by the Weltheim Company in 1665, and in 1626 at Dresden. Thus early, then, do we know it to have been acted, and it may have been acted earlier. How the text stood in either 1778 or 1665 we have no means of knowing.

" Titus Andronicus " we can trace farther back. It was acted in 1600; printed 1620; re-printed 1626. Here the doctrine of anything like gradual degradation is out of the question, since the time is too short for it; though for an intentional alteration it is amply sufficient. The instance, however, of " Titus Audronicus" is of little practical value. Whatever we may say about our openness to conviction, it is certain we shall not apply the same rule of evidence to the two questions. With " Hamlet " we shall claim for Shakespear the *maximum* of authorship ; with " Titus Andronicus " the *minimum*. The reader, however, who finds himself thus playing fast-

and-loose with his *data*, should distrust his judgment.

"Titus Andronicus," however, is not the only play that bears upon the question. In the "Taming of the Shrew" we have what the "Bestrafte Brudermord" is supposed to be; viz., an actual accommodation of a Shakespearian play to a German audience. How is this effected? Not on the principle of omitting the best passages of the play, but on that of adding to them, developing them, or, in the opinion of the adapter, improving them. Thus, in the place of the Induction we have a Prologue spoken by the Patient Job. Then the names of the Dramatis Personæ, are Germanized; Katherine being called *Jungfer Catharina Hurleputz*, *Bianca*, *Jungfer Sabina*, *Süsmäulchen*, and so on throughout the list. Then there is a musical scene, *Singenspiel*. Finally, though the play is manifestly Shakespearian, the author does not even know that it is English.

And this anticipates an objection. It may be asked, whether it is likely that, after the establishment of Shakespear's reputation, bad copies, and rough drafts, would be preferred to dramas which he had put in the best form of which they were susceptible; or whether the compositions by so conspicuous a dramatist could be mistaken for those of an obscure one. The answer is clear. Whatever may be the presumptions to the contrary, in the case of the "Taming of the Shrew" such an error of judgment actually occurs.

ERRATA.

Page 8. Note; after " Scriptores " *add* " Rerum Danicarum."

„ 76. " Within . . . . years " *fill up* " a hundred and twenty."

„ 77. " Within . . . . years " *fill up* " a hundred and twenty."

„ 78. " In A.D. 9 . ." *fill up* " 950."

„ 89. *For* " Rest " *read* " Wit."

„ 90. *For* " Ames " *read* " Meres."

„ 93. " The ursurper then being . . ." *fill up* " Godard."